THE GRASS IS GREENER

A Comedy in Two Acts

by

HUGH AND MARGARET WILLIAMS

Copyright © 1960 by Hugh and Margaret Williams
Originally published 1960 by Evans Brothers Ltd
All Rights Reserved

THE GRASS IS GREENER is fully protected under the copyright laws of the British Commonwealth, including Canada, the United States of America, and all other countries of the Copyright Union. All rights, including professional and amateur stage productions, recitation, lecturing, public reading, motion picture, radio broadcasting, television and the rights of translation into foreign languages are strictly reserved.

ISBN 978-0-573-11596-7

www.samuelfrench.co.uk
www.samuelfrench.com

FOR AMATEUR PRODUCTION ENQUIRIES

UNITED KINGDOM AND WORLD
EXCLUDING NORTH AMERICA
plays@samuelfrench.co.uk
020 7255 4302/01

Each title is subject to availability from Samuel French, depending upon country of performance.

CAUTION: Professional and amateur producers are hereby warned that *THE GRASS IS GREENER* is subject to a licensing fee. Publication of this play does not imply availability for performance. Both amateurs and professionals considering a production are strongly advised to apply to the appropriate agent before starting rehearsals, advertising, or booking a theatre. A licensing fee must be paid whether the title is presented for charity or gain and whether or not admission is charged.

The Amateur Rights in this play are controlled by Samuel French Ltd, 24-32 Stephenson Way, London NW1 2HD.

No one shall make any changes in this title for the purpose of production. No part of this book may be reproduced, stored in a retrieval system, or transmitted in any form, by any means, now known or yet to be invented, including mechanical, electronic, photocopying, recording, videotaping, or otherwise, without the prior written permission of the publisher. No one shall upload this title, or part of this title, to any social media websites.

The right of Hugh and Margaret Williams to be identified as authors of this work has been asserted in accordance with Section 77 of the Copyright, Designs and Patents Act 1988.

The Grass is Greener

This play was first produced at the St. Martin's Theatre, London, on 2nd December 1956, with the following cast:—

VICTOR	Hugh Williams
SELLARS	Moray Watson
HILARY	Celia Johnson
CHARLES	Edward Underdown
HATTIE	Joan Greenwood

The play was directed by JACK MINSTER, with décor by HUTCHINSON SCOTT.

The action of the play takes place in a house in Hampshire in the month of May.

ACT ONE
SCENE 1	A Friday afternoon
SCENE 2	A week later

ACT TWO
SCENE 1	The following evening
SCENE 2	Later that night

No character in this play is intended to represent any person, alive or dead.

NOTE: *Running time of this play, excluding intervals, is approximately one hour and fifty-five minutes.*

PRODUCTION NOTE

WHEN the curtain rises there should be a not too obtrusive murmur of voices as of a party being shown round the house. Presumably, they have just reached and are passing the private rooms in which the Rhyalls live. We see a very attractive and comfortable part of their living room. The noise dies away as Victor closes the door and is heard only once again when Hilary has her short telephone conversation. In London we had these sounds recorded. This is not really necessary, however; but on each of the two occasions the noise should be recognizably similar, as the same things are probably being said by the guide and the reactions are likely to be the same.

The room should be full of spring sunlight and mellow and very lived-in. Soon after Hilary's entrance, Victor says to her that spring is a turbulent season and warns her that as one grows older the fiercer and more poignant it becomes. She replies that she finds it very disturbing and already a possible complication for one or other of them is sign-posted. Romance is about again.

The play should be played with a light gravity. It is high comedy; and breadth of playing, working for laughs or milking of situations should be eschewed. David Garrick is quoted as saying that you can fool the town with Tragedy, but Comedy is a serious business. When after Victor's exit at the end of Act One, Scene 1, Hilary tells Charles that he (Victor) "is not usually as facetious as that" it is merely the word she appears to choose being anxious and perhaps a little put out. Victor has not played the scene facetiously, but rather with a mock-seriousness, and with a hint of banter, yet always with good manners as well as with style.

The play deals in jealousy, possessiveness, apprehension, self-doubt, loneliness comedically rather than dramatically, and while we laugh we think a little, too, for wit has an edge to its humour. The duel in the final scene has a touch of cloak-and-dagger romance about it—mock heroics—but never insincere.

Should the actress who plays Hattie have seen Miss Greenwood play the part, she would be wise not to attempt an echo of her performance, but rather to make it quite her own, and to be good, amusing and gay entirely in *her* way and no other. One can emulate a performance but

PRODUCTION NOTE

not a personality—and, here, amusing as the performance was, the personality was very strong. Imitation can only be reach-me-down. In fact, the only wise thing for the producer to do is to give the part to the actress at his disposal who has the most amusing personality, provided that she is suitable in other ways.

The lighting in the second scene of Act One is almost the same as in the first, except that it is a shade later in the day. The first scene of the second act opens with the acting area round the sofa and mantelpiece lit for the evening, the rest of the lights being added by Sellars on his first exit. The final scene opens with only the passage light showing Charles, and the full lighting coming up after the shooting on Sellars' entrance, which follows that of Charles and Victor, the passage light being extinguished at the same time.

It merely remains for me to wish you luck with the production whenever it is done, and to suggest as with all plays that send an audience away pleased and with their spirits raised a little that you, too, should seem to have enjoyed yourselves while acting it—as no doubt you will, in fact, have done—for it is a charming and delightful and amusing play.

JACK MINSTER

CHARACTERS
in order of appearance

    Victor

    Sellars

    Hilary

    Charles

    Hattie

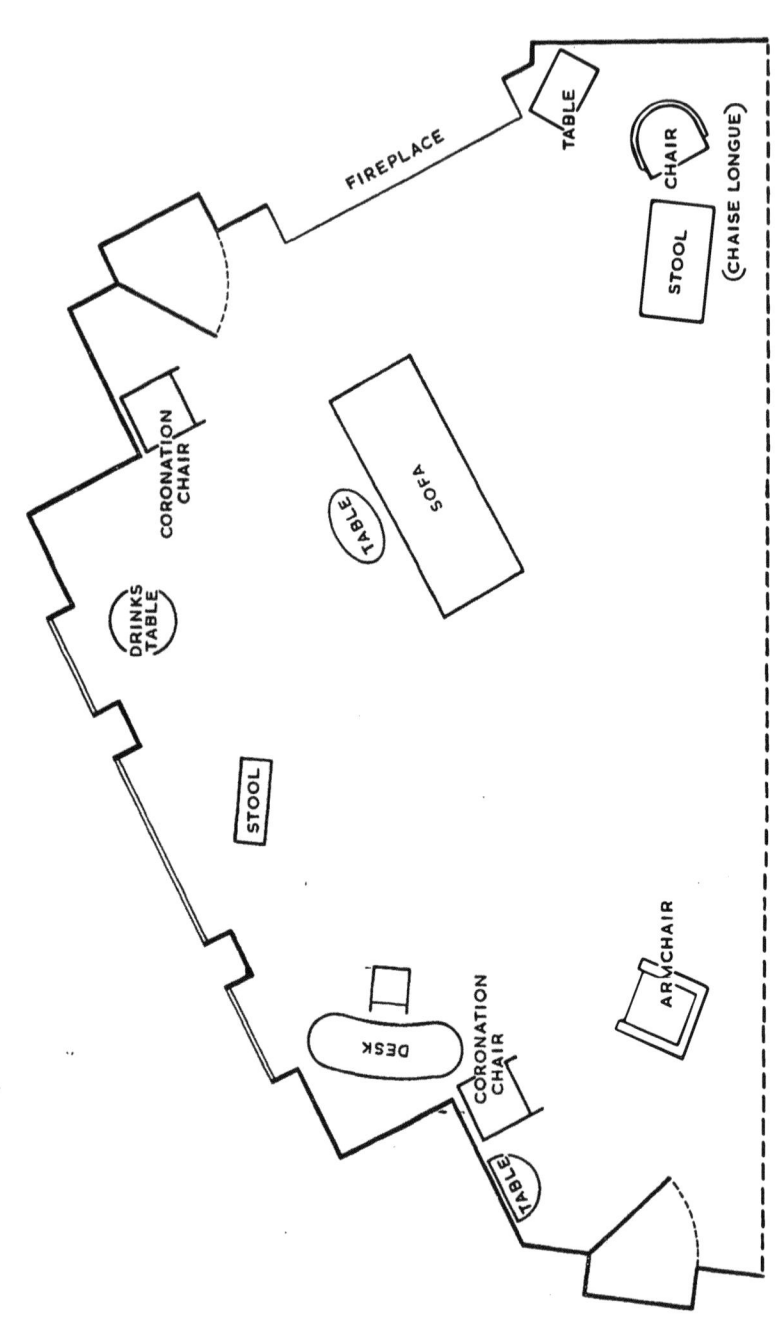

*THE GRASS IS GREENER

ACT ONE

SCENE I

The curtain rises on a small, charming upstairs sitting room in the private part of one of the stately homes of England. Through the long windows, which face the audience, can be seen the dark branches of a cedar tree. It is early spring.

There is a door on the L. which leads to the parts of the house open to the public, and another on the R. leading to the wing occupied by the family.

A large flat writing table is prominent on the right-hand side of the room, comfortable sofas and armchairs, a drink table, and a beautiful fireplace. The general appearance and atmosphere of the room has probably not changed greatly in the last two hundred years.

Gay spring sunlight is pouring through the long windows. It is a beautiful little room, but also comfortable and rather cosy.

>   VICTOR is seated at the writing table doing his accounts. He is a nice looking man, attractive, and dealing with middle age as he does with everything else—with skill and assurance.
>
>   The door to the public rooms is open and voices can be heard of people being shown round.
>
>   VICTOR rises and shuts the door. As he crosses back to the desk the telephone rings. He picks up the receiver.

VICTOR. Good afternoon. Yes it is. Oh, hullo, Vicar, how are you? Good. And Mrs. Jordan? Good. Yes, it's a lovely day, isn't it—real spring. I suppose you want to give me the Lessons for Sunday? Just a second, I'll jot it down. Deuteronomy chapter twenty-eight, from the beginning—down to the fifteenth verse. O.K., and the second?
(*He continues writing.*) Matthew—yes—yes. That sounds a long one—you promised me no long ones. It isn't? I suppose I shall have to believe you. Is it all right if I drop the altar flowers in to you tomorrow morning? I won't cut 'em till then. Tell Mrs. Jordan I'm

---

*It is illegal to perform this play, *in any circumstances whatsoever*, without a licence. Please refer, for full details, to Copyright Notice preceding main text. *Copyright Act 1956.*

going to bring her round some tulips. See you then. Good-bye. (*He sits in desk chair and starts doing his accounts again.*)
(*Enter* SELLARS, *the butler. Though dressed conventionally, his face is a little too intellectual for a butler, consequently his appearance is not so much disappointing as disarming. He seems a little out of character, which indeed he is. He crosses to* R. *side of desk, facing* VICTOR.)

SELLARS. Am I disturbing you, milord?

VICTOR. Yes, you are, Sellars.

SELLARS. I'm sorry, milord. (*He is not prepared to leave however and moves round above desk to behind* VICTOR *and level with him.*)

VICTOR. You've made me forget what one hundred and forty-three half-crowns are. Eights into one hundred and forty-three—

SELLARS. I make it seventeen pounds seventeen and six. I wonder if I might have a word with you.

VICTOR (*pleased*). So do I. So we're probably right. Not bad. Not bad at all, considering last Saturday wasn't a very nice day. (*Turns to face* SELLARS *and picks up a booklet from desk.*) Funny, the Saturday people don't buy a booklet, only fourteen copies, disappointing!

SELLARS. They're very good on teas, milord.

VICTOR. Yes, and more profit on teas than the booklet, so we mustn't grumble. I always feel a little hurt when they don't buy the booklet. I thought you and I wrote it rather well. Of course what we really want is a licence.

SELLARS. A wine and spirits licence, milord?

VICTOR. M'm. And beer of course.

SELLARS. Wouldn't that attract the wrong sort of people?

VICTOR. If the riff-raff who parade through my house and gardens leaving nut shells and apple cores all over the place are the right kind, I'd just as soon have my privacy invaded by the other sort. The possible eventualities I incur, through allowing the public into my house, make me very jumpy.

SELLARS. In what way?

VICTOR. Supposing someone slid down the banisters and broke a hip. (SELLARS *breaks* U.S. *a little.*) Anything could happen really.

SELLARS (*back to level with* VICTOR). I should have thought a licence would encourage that sort of thing, milord.

VICTOR. I dare say. It was only a thought. An attempt to be enterprising. I got the idea the other day when I passed a pub called "The Duke of Bedford". How much is fourteen one and sixes?

SELLARS. A guinea, milord.

VICTOR. How charming. Now I can't do my accounts with you standing there. What do you want?
SELLARS. I beg your pardon, milord, I came to ask if you'd finished with "The Times".
VICTOR. Yes, I think so, why? (*He starts putting three full bags of half-crowns into the big money bag.*)
SELLARS. Then would you mind if I took it now, milord?
VICTOR. What do you want "The Times" for—to light a fire? What do you want to light a fire for? Much too warm for a fire.
SELLARS. I want to read it.
VICTOR. Oh! Yes of course—by all means. It's about somewhere. (*He returns to his accounts.*)
SELLARS (*crosses above sofa looking for "The Times"*). Doesn't it strike you as a little odd, milord, that your butler should want to borrow "The Times" in the middle of a Friday afternoon? When his day off is on Thursday, I mean.
VICTOR (*putting loose half-crowns into empty bag*). I hadn't really thought about it. Yes, I suppose it does. What's the matter—you bored?
SELLARS (*picks up "The Times" from floor at* L. *end of sofa*). To death, milord.
VICTOR. Why aren't you working?
SELLARS. I haven't any work to do.
VICTOR. How's that?
SELLARS. I've done the silver. I've nothing to do now until I serve your tea at four-thirty.
VICTOR. No, no, no, I didn't mean that sort of work, I meant your novel. Why aren't you working on that?
SELLARS. I'm stuck badly. I nearly tore the whole thing up last night.
VICTOR (*disengaging himself from his work for the first time*). Now you mustn't do that. (*He leans back, looking at* SELLARS. *He has some half-crowns in one hand and a money bag in the other.*) What's the trouble?
SELLARS (*to below sofa*). Almost certainly the basic trouble is myself. I'm fundamentally happy and contented. That's bad enough of course, but on top of that I'm normal. That's fatal.
VICTOR. D'you mean you'd prefer to be unhappy and abnormal? (*Putting money into bag and keeping four half-crowns in his hand.*)
SELLARS. But of course! (*Round* D.R. *end of sofa.*) I want to be a success. And to be a success one must at least start off by being contemporary, which unfortunately I'm not. (VICTOR *puts money bag into big bag.*)

It means I've no feeling of insecurity or frustration—no despair. (*Back to level with* VICTOR.)

VICTOR. And that's essential?

SELLARS. The first essential. And I feel perfectly contented—really rather blameless. And hardly resent anything at all.

VICTOR. Oh, Lord. (*He puts the big bag away in desk drawer except for the four half-crowns which go in his pocket.*) But you must have known all this when you chucked teaching to become a writer.

SELLARS (*turns to face* VICTOR). I don't think I did chuck it to become a writer. Oh, don't misunderstand me, I want to write, but I don't think that was the real reason I gave up teaching.

(VICTOR *rises and crosses below sofa to fireplace. He takes a board with a lot of lists on it from mantelpiece and crosses back to below sofa.*)

VICTOR. Then you're here under false pretences. You answered my advertisement, and when I asked you what your real qualifications were, you said you held a degree in science. Despite such a ludicrous recommendation I engaged you as my butler, partly because you said you wanted to write a novel, and you couldn't write after teaching all day, and partly because I remembered your father when he was butler, and a very good one, too, I always understood. (*Sits on* R. *arm of sofa.*) Luckily it's turned out very well. I'd like to know what your reason was if it wasn't to write. Were you sick of teaching?

SELLARS. No. (*Pause.*) I began to disapprove of what I taught. I began to disapprove of science.

VICTOR. I beg your pardon?

SELLARS. I maintain that scientific progress has gone too far too quickly. As Bertrand Russell said "Science has outstripped wisdom". I felt— I felt—well simply I felt I couldn't go on teaching it any more. Perhaps disapprove is the wrong word.

VICTOR. Is distrust the right one?

SELLARS (*nodding*). Maybe it is.

VICTOR. Yes, I see.

SELLARS. But you're quite right, milord, I am here under false pretences, and it worries me—a great deal.

VICTOR. How d'you mean?

SELLARS. Well, milord, the point is I feel such a waste of money. I don't really think you should have a butler at all.

VICTOR. Oh really.

SELLARS. I don't mean to be impertinent, but—

VICTOR. Go on, in for a penny in for a pound.
SELLARS (*taking the plunge*). You see, milord, you're not contemporary, either.
VICTOR. You mean I'm an antique?
SELLARS. No, milord, you're traditional.
VICTOR. Well, go on.
SELLARS. Ever since your family first lived in this house, they've always had butlers—in earlier times I suppose they called them stewards. From your point of view that's sufficient reason to have one now. But don't you see, milord, nowadays you don't need one? Really you don't. There's no work for me. (*Crosses below* VICTOR *and wanders right round sofa.*) Years ago when there were big families, and entertaining was part of the life of a great house, and the whole place was occupied, and it was open house to your friends and not just the public—then my job must have been fun, and very hard work. But today—today, I've really nothing to do. (*Back to level with* VICTOR.) And I— and I—
VICTOR (*who has been listening attentively.*) What, Sellars?
SELLARS. I should feel much happier, if you'd either sack me or reduce my wages by three pounds a week. (*There is a pause.*) That's what I came in here to say, milord, not really to borrow "The Times".
VICTOR. Yes, I see. (*He crosses below* SELLARS. *He puts the board of lists in a desk drawer, then goes on round* R. *side of desk to behind sofa.*) What you're saying, in effect, is that I'm out of date, old fashioned, and clinging to a way of life that's had dry rot in it since nineteen thirty-eight. (*Takes cigarette from packet in his pocket.*)
SELLARS. No, I didn't say that.
VICTOR (*by chaise longue*). Well, you're wrong. You've never been so wrong in all your born days. And I'll tell you why you're wrong. This house and these lands may be mine in title, but I regard them as a small part of England that I hold in trust—in trust for the future, not for my son. I find that fascinating and stimulating. There are treasures, and beauty, and history in this house, and I'm preserving them in the most modern, streamline, commercial way it's possible to do. The farm pays, the market garden pays, the hens pay, and her Ladyship's mushrooms pay.
SELLARS. Yes, I do see all that. (*Crosses below sofa to light* VICTOR'S *cigarette with matches from his pocket.*)
VICTOR. And the reason I employ you is because I know jolly well the two-and-sixpenny public are far more thrilled by catching a glimpse

of a real live butler than they are by the Velasquez at the top of the staircase. In spite of what you may think to the contrary (*Sits on edge of chaise longue.*) I am, in fact, extremely contemporary, highly efficient, and very businesslike. And to prove it to you, I'll accept your offer and reduce your wages by three pounds a week as from next Monday.

(*Enter* HILARY D.R. *She is younger than* VICTOR *and beautiful by any standards; she has remained soft and sweet and unspoiled and her husband, quite rightly, loves her very much. She is carrying gardening gloves and she crosses up to* R. *side of desk.*)

And now I suggest you go and teach your grandmother to suck eggs.

HILARY (*putting on her shoes which are under* U.S. *end of desk*). No he can't. I want Sellars to do something for me. (*To* SELLARS.) Would you do the mushroom run for me? They're all ready packed now, but as long as you have them at the station by six-thirty.

SELLARS (*crosses below sofa to* D.R. *door*). Certainly, milady.

HILARY (*crossing above sofa table to fireplace*). And I think the van wants petrol, so watch out. Get five gallons at Pickards. My account, remember. It's getting towards the end of the month and I want to hot it up a bit. (*Takes off her jacket and throws it over the chaise longue.*)

SELLARS. Very good, milady. (*Turns to go.*)

VICTOR (*rising and crossing below sofa to desk*). Sellars, how many half-crowns in three pounds?

SELLARS. About a bus load, milord. (*Exit.*)

VICTOR (*sits desk chair, laughing*). You know I like him more and more. He's that rare being—a man who obeys the dictates of his conscience.

HILARY. What are you talking about?

VICTOR. About what he and I were talking about.

HILARY (*puts gloves in drawer of sofa table*). And what was that?

VICTOR. You could call it progress, I suppose.

HILARY. You know, I've been wondering.

VICTOR. What, my love?

HILARY (*up to* C. *window*). D'you think he liked teaching?

VICTOR. I think so, why?

HILARY. I wonder if he misses it.

VICTOR. He said he was bored just now. Maybe he does. What's all this leading up to?

HILARY. D'you think if I was terribly clever with him, he'd give Emma her lessons?

VICTOR. Give Emma her lessons! Have you gone out of your mind?
HILARY. Only from nine-thirty to twelve.
VICTOR. He's a butler, not a governess.
HILARY. It would mean we needn't have a governess. (*Down* R. *of sofa to sit on* R. *arm*.) Emma's no trouble now, I can manage her perfectly well. It's simply a question of her lessons.
VICTOR. You mean sack Miss Mathews?
HILARY. Yes.
VICTOR. D'you know something?
HILARY. What?
VICTOR. I adore you.
HILARY. Do you, my darling? I'm so glad.
VICTOR. And I think that's the most bloody marvellous idea you've ever had in your whole life.
HILARY. We'd have to give him a little something extra, I suppose.
VICTOR. We'll give him three pounds a week extra.
HILARY. Then you approve?
VICTOR. My dear girl, if we sack Miss Mathews and sell the television we'd return to a civilized way of life. What a pity we can't sell Miss Mathews. (*He picks up* "*A.B.C.*") When can she leave? Let's look up a train.
HILARY. Yes, that's always fun. (*Rises and crosses to* D.R. *door*.)
VICTOR (*a sudden thought*). But d'you think he will?
HILARY. Sellars? If Emma and I work on him right he will. (*Exit* D.R. *Pause. Off*.) Darling. (*Enters to just inside door with a copy of* "*Henley*".)
VICTOR. What?
HILARY. I'm sorry, but I want to work on you, too.
VICTOR. Very unlike you, to warn me.
HILARY (*shutting door*). Don't be beastly.
VICTOR (*looking at her affectionately*). Beauty and the beastly.
HILARY. Thank you, darling, how good you are to me!
VICTOR. To you or for you?
HILARY. Both, I'm happy to say.
VICTOR. Then you're lucky, aren't you?
HILARY (*just below* R. *end of sofa she turns* D.S. *to* VICTOR). Very lucky.
VICTOR. What are you reading?
HILARY. I wanted to look something up.
VICTOR. What?
HILARY. "Henley."

VICTOR. Why?

HILARY (*at* L. *end of sofa*). Look out of the window and you'll know why. (VICTOR *rises up to* C. *window*.) I always want to read it at this time of year. Here it is. (*Reads*.)

> And it's O, the wild Spring and his chances
> And dreams!
> There's a life in the blood—
> O, this gracious, and thirsting, and aching
> Unrest!
> All life's at the bud,
> And my heart, full of April, is breaking
> My breast.

VICTOR (*who has never taken his eyes away from her, crosses back to desk and sits*). It's May. The ninth. At least that's the date I shall put on your cheque.

HILARY (*to above sofa table*). Who said anything about a cheque?

VICTOR (*taking cheque book from desk drawer*). "This gracious, and thirsting, and aching unrest." That can only mean one thing, my darling. New clothes. (*Writing cheque*.)

HILARY (*leans* L. *pillar of* C. *window, back to audience*). You are clever, aren't you?

VICTOR. On the contrary you're the one who's clever. Spring! It's a turbulent season. All the clatter of re-birth.

HILARY. New nests and young grass. Song birds rehearsing and green leaves sprouting yellow. It's powerful stuff, and rather overwhelming.

(VICTOR *rises with cheque to* L. *of* HILARY, *pacing* D.S. *a bit*.)

VICTOR. Why did the bulrush? Because the cowslips out. Nature playing mothers and fathers.

HILARY. Then she should be more modest about it and keep it to herself. Why drag me in? It's not fair and I don't like it. I find it very disturbing.

VICTOR. I must warn you, my darling, the older you get the fiercer and more poignant the spring becomes.

HILARY. It's quite merciless, isn't it? One almost longs for the sanctuary of autumn.

VICTOR. Except for asparagus I couldn't agree with you more. (*Handing her the cheque*.) Here you are. (*Breaks* L. *to* L. *end of sofa*.)

HILARY (*turns to him*). No, I don't want a cheque from you, I didn't

mean that, honestly I didn't. I just wanted to ask you if I could spend some of my mushroom money.
VICTOR. I don't allow you to accept money from other mushrooms.
HILARY (L. *of desk chair*). You've put "with love" above your signature.
VICTOR (*crossing below sofa to* D.R. *door*). That's all right, I've initialled it.
HILARY (*down to level with him*). Don't go.
VICTOR. I'm busy.
HILARY. I haven't thanked you yet.
VICTOR. You don't have to.
HILARY. Where are you going?
VICTOR. To kiss good-bye to Miss Mathews. (*Exit.*)
    (HILARY *smiles happily, puts the cheque in her pocket, and crosses to the window. She picks up the copy of "Henley", starts to go and is stopped by the telephone ringing. She crosses up to telephone* R. *of the desk and answers it, leaning on* R. *edge of desk facing the fireplace.*)
HILARY. Hullo! Yes. Oh, hullo, Margot, how are you? Fine, thanks—yes, I'm sure she'd love to, on the twentieth, yes I think that's all right. Three-thirty— What? Oh no! Oh Lord, must it be fancy dress? Yes, I know they love it, but God, it's a bore. Whatever Emma goes as there are always four others. No, no, no—I'll manage something. I might turn her bridesmaid's dress into Little Miss Muffet. That'll mean a spider. A conjurer— Oh my dear, she'll be thrilled. We'll see you then, if not before. How's Ronnie? Give him our love. Yes indeed she'll be looking forward to it. Thank you so much. Good-bye. (*She puts down the receiver.*) Good-bye, good-bye, good-bye.
    (HILARY *crosses to pick up her jacket, then crosses to door* R., *as the other door* L., *leading to the public part of the house, opens quietly and* CHARLES *enters. He is an attractive, charming and well dressed American in his early forties. He has a camera slung over his shoulder, and carries in one hand his hat and a small booklet.*)
CHARLES (*entering to just inside door and leaving it half open*). I'm awfully sorry. I guess I've intruded.
HILARY (*after a slight pause while she looks at him*). Yes, you have, haven't you?
CHARLES. I was making the tour of the house and got kind of absorbed in this little book. I should have gone on down the corridor, I guess, but I made a mistake and took the wrong turning.
HILARY. I don't call opening a door marked "Private" making a mistake. I call it trespassing.

CHARLES (*after a pause. They are summing each other up*). What are you going to do, prosecute me? If you are I shall defend the action, because there is no notice on this door saying "Private".
HILARY. Oh yes there is. (CHARLES *opens the door a little wider to show her there is no notice on it.*) Oh, I beg your pardon.
CHARLES. I'm the one that's begging your pardon. For intruding, ma'am.
HILARY. Someone must have taken it down.
CHARLES. Yes, ma'am.
HILARY. And in England we only call the Queen ma'am.
CHARLES. In the United States we make up for having no royalty by calling everybody ma'am. (*His charm is working.*)
　　　(HILARY *throws her coat over back of armchair crossing, below sofa to fireplace still holding book. She sees "Private" notice on floor outside door.*)
HILARY. Now perhaps you'll be good enough to put it back.
CHARLES (*innocently*). Put what back?
HILARY. The notice you removed from the door. There it is on the floor.
CHARLES. Must have fallen down.
HILARY. Rubbish. You put it there.
CHARLES (*pinning the notice back*). Well, if I'd put it in my pocket I might have taken it away with me.
HILARY. The police would describe your actions as "entering with intent".
CHARLES (*smiling*). I guess I did enter with intent at that. Not to steal anything. (*Crosses to above sofa table.*)
HILARY. I think I deserve an explanation.
CHARLES. It's quite simple, really. I'm just naturally sort of bad at resisting temptation. I'd spent a wonderful hour going over your beautiful home—
HILARY. You mean house, don't you? (*She crosses below sofa to just above on-stage edge of arm-chair.*) You can't call a place a home when people only have to pay half a crown to walk all over it. And not content with seeing the public rooms you wanted to see the private ones as well. Is that it?
CHARLES (*takes one step to above* R. *end of sofa table*). Let's say I was curious to see the people who live in them.
HILARY. Nowadays an Englishman's home is no longer his castle—it's his income. It's unfair of you to take advantage of it.

CHARLES. You're making me feel rather ashamed of myself.
HILARY. That's the price you must expect to pay if you give way to temptation.
CHARLES (*a little contrite*). I really am awfully sorry. I don't know how to forgive myself.
HILARY. Surely I'm the person who has to forgive you.
CHARLES. Yes, ma'am. I'm sorry, no, ma'am. No I don't mean—no, ma'am, I just remembered not to say ma'am, that's all. You've got me really worried.
HILARY. Well, don't worry any more.
CHARLES. Thank you.

(*There is a pause while they look at each other. They do not realize it quite yet, but they are falling in love.*)

You are Lady Rhyall, aren't you?

(HILARY *nods, and he drops down* R. *of sofa to level with her. He holds out his hand to her.*)

I'm very happy to know you.
HILARY (*drops "Henley" in armchair and shakes hands*). How d'you do?
CHARLES. Yes, you sort of have to be, don't you.
HILARY. Have to be what?
CHARLES. The Countess of Rhyall.
HILARY. Why?
CHARLES. You're the perfect type casting.
HILARY. Don't tell me you're in the film industry?
CHARLES. No, God forbid. I'm an oil man.
HILARY. Oh, you're a millionaire!
CHARLES (*nodding*). Yes I am.
HILARY. Oh well, won't you sit down?
CHARLES. Thank you. (*He puts hat and camera on desk, booklet in* L. *pocket and sits* R. *arm of sofa.*) Why d'you take it so for granted I'm a millionaire?
HILARY (*sits at desk chair, pulling it round to face audience*). Nearly all the Americans I meet seem to be. Especially the oily ones.
CHARLES. I hoped you'd be impressed.
HILARY. As a matter of fact I am—just a little. (*Pause.*) Have you been a millionaire quite some time?
CHARLES. I guess I have at that.
HILARY. Never resisting a temptation from one year's end to the other.
CHARLES. Is that how I seem to you?

HILARY. No, I can't honestly say it is. Why d'you think I'm type casting?
CHARLES (*choosing his words carefully*). Because you're cool—and elegant, and at ease and—and—
HILARY. And what?
CHARLES. And very lovely.
HILARY (*rises and crosses below sofa up to* U.L. *door*). I suppose the reason you're a millionaire is because you insist on value for money. You're certainly getting your half a crown's worth, aren't you? (*Shuts door.*)
CHARLES (*rises*). I'm an American—I say what I think.
HILARY. And hesitate before you say it. A Frenchman would never have hesitated.
CHARLES. And an Englishman?
HILARY (*back* L. *of sofa to below it*). An Englishman would never have said it.
CHARLES. You mean an Englishman wouldn't tell a married woman she was lovely?
HILARY. Oh no! I don't mean that. It's just that he usually tells the husband first.
   (HILARY *sits* L. *end of sofa and* CHARLES *sits* R. *arm of sofa.*)
CHARLES. What's the point of that?
HILARY. He knows the husband will repeat it to the wife. (*Imitating the English husband.*) "D'you know what old George said to me tonight, my dear? Said he thought you looked lovely."
CHARLES. I said very lovely.
HILARY. The wife's intrigued, and the next time she's alone with George she sees to it he tells her himself. It's an oblique approach but not a bad one. It's effective, so I understand.
CHARLES. But I don't know your husband, and my name isn't George.
HILARY. What is it, Theodore or Harry or Dwight? They're the only American names I know, I'm afraid. Oh! And Bing. It would be too good to be true if you were Bing!
CHARLES. Charles. What's yours?
HILARY. Hilary.
CHARLES. Hilary. That's a boy's name. You don't look like a boy to me.
HILARY. And a term.
CHARLES. A term for what?
HILARY. The Lent term—at Oxford. Charles what?
CHARLES. Delacro. D-E-L-A-C-R-O.
HILARY. It sounds French.

CHARLES. It is. It's really Delacroix. C-R-O-I-X. But we're a simple, straightforward people in the United States and when we see an X on the end of a name we pronounce it. My grandfather thought Delacroix (*He pronounces the X.*) sounded like a duck laying an egg, so he cut it off. The X, I mean. He was born in France. Near Tours.

HILARY. Now isn't that odd! I had a French grandfather, and he lived in the Touraine. Perhaps we're cousins.

CHARLES. I doubt that. Your grandfather was probably a nobleman—mine was a clockmaker.

HILARY. Now you're a millionaire and I'm a mushroom grower. Well, there you are! That's how the world wags.

(*Another silence, which she eventually breaks.*)

(*Rises to fireplace facing* CHARLES.) It's too early to offer you a cup of tea, perhaps you'd like a drink?

CHARLES. I don't really want one, but if taking a drink off you means I'm now your guest and not just an intruder, then I certainly will.

HILARY. Let's just say it's because our grandfathers were compatriots. Will you help yourself?

CHARLES. Thank you. (*Rises to R. end of sofa.*)

HILARY. It's something you're quite accustomed to, I imagine.

CHARLES. Helping myself?

(*She nods.*)

Is that a crack or a compliment?

HILARY. Which would you say it was?

CHARLES. In my country I'd say it was a compliment. In yours I guess it's a crack. And if you'll forgive my saying so, I think that's a pity. (*He is helping himself to a gin and tonic.*)

HILARY. I'm not in a position to argue, the relative value of mushrooms and oil in the world market being so unfairly what it is. And don't try and turn the tables on me.

CHARLES. Why not?

HILARY. Because I don't like it.

CHARLES. Because you're not accustomed to it?

HILARY. No, I'm not.

CHARLES. Then I apologize. Some of your English customs I find more unusual than others. Having no ice in my drinks of course I'm quite used to.

HILARY. Damn! I'm most awfully sorry. (*Moving towards the bell.*) I'll get some in two minutes.

CHARLES. No. Please, really, I don't want any. I never complain unless it actually burns my tongue. Can I fix you a drink?

HILARY. Fix! Sounds as if you were going to drug me.

CHARLES. Sometimes I think the greatest barrier between our two countries is the bond of a common language. Can I pour you out a drink?

HILARY. No, thank you.

CHARLES (*round* R. *end of sofa to below it with gin and tonic*). My French is pretty limited, too, but I believe I get on better over there than I can here. Tell me, why do you grow mushrooms—to make omelettes?

HILARY. To make money. (*She indicates him to sit and drops to* C. *of fireplace.*)

CHARLES. And do you?

HILARY. Oh yes. It's rather fun, isn't it? Making money, I mean. (*Drops to chaise longue, sits at on-stage end facing him.*)

CHARLES (*sits* R. *end of sofa*). Not for me it wasn't. I had to work too hard. I'm having my fun now.

HILARY. And what fun d'you have?

CHARLES. I travel. I fish. I've just had a week's fishing now, with a friend of mine who has a beat on the Hampshire Avon. I was driving back to London when I remembered Lynley Hall was on the way.

HILARY. What else?

CHARLES. What else? I guess I try to understand what I see, and grasp what I listen to. I watch the world bumping along and try to make some sense of it. Very small sections of it I try to help. I like to sail. I like to play bridge. I'm a balletomane, and I enjoy the theatre. I try to make a reasonable pattern out of my life, and not let it be just a crazy mixed up doodle.

HILARY. And ever since you read Churchill's little book about it, you've been trying to paint.

CHARLES. Well, what d'you know! That's absolutely right.

HILARY. And where do you live?

CHARLES. I have a home in Long Island, but I'm only there a couple of months a year.

HILARY. There you go again, calling a house a home. It can't be much of a home if you're only there two months out of the twelve.

CHARLES. I guess you're right.

HILARY. And you're divorced. (*There is no question mark to this.*)

CHARLES. Yes, I am. My wife and I divorced three years ago. Maybe if we hadn't I'd have a home and not just a house. Why were you so sure I was divorced?
HILARY. You're the perfect type casting.
(*They laugh, and then another silence captures their conversation.*)
And I bet you go to a psychiatrist, and take tranquilisers, and are frightened of ulcers—and eat too many salads.
CHARLES. Lady Rhyall's report on the social activities of the American male.
HILARY (*rises and crosses below sofa to* R.C.). You subscribe to the "Reader's Digest", belong to the Racquets Club, and worked your way through college. Or did you get a football scholarship?
CHARLES. No, I worked my way through college. (*Moves to* L. *end of sofa.*) As a crooner, believe it or not.
HILARY (*leans on* L. *edge of desk chair facing him*). And played half back on the football team.
CHARLES. Correct.
HILARY. And were in the Marines during the war.
CHARLES. Army Air Force.
HILARY. And finished up a colonel.
CHARLES. Wrong again. A one-star general. Anything else?
HILARY. You call your girl friends either "Honey" or "Sugar".
CHARLES. Isn't it my turn to be rude to you, now?
HILARY. And if you hadn't got a camera slung round you, you wouldn't feel properly dressed.
CHARLES. Like a Britisher wears his umbrella?
HILARY. That's our climate.
CHARLES. D'you mean they're actually constructed to unroll? I thought they were just for hailing taxis.
HILARY. We unroll them watching cricket and at most weddings. (*Sits* R. *arm of sofa.*) All right, I'll be fair. You can have your turn now. Being rude to me, I mean.
(CHARLES *is looking at her, and absorbed in what he sees.*)
Well, go on. Begin.
CHARLES (*puts glass on sofa table*). Well, now let me see. I'd say you were an only child and were very spoilt, and you were called Hilary because your mother and father were disappointed you weren't a boy.
HILARY. I have three brothers.

CHARLES. Ah well, they spoilt you.

HILARY. They bullied me, teased me, tricked me out of my pocket money, cut my head open and destroyed my belief in Father Christmas. And I simply adored them. I was called Hilary after someone my father hoped would leave me something in his will, but he never did.

CHARLES. You wore a brace on your teeth and were always considered the ugly duckling.

(*She nods.*)
And then turned out the deb' of the year.

HILARY. You're doing quite nicely, aren't you? You must be in practice.

CHARLES. No, this is your game. I've never played before. Were you the deb' of the year?

HILARY. No.

CHARLES. Anyway, that didn't bother you because all you really wanted was to go up to Oxford.

HILARY. Cambridge.

CHARLES. Forgive me. Of course—Cambridge. A light blue stocking, and much more attractive. You majored history and can finish "The Times" crossword over your breakfast.

HILARY. Yes and no.

CHARLES. What d'you mean, yes and no?

HILARY. I mean yes, I read history at Cambridge; and no, I read the "Daily Herald" at breakfast.

CHARLES. Don't tell me you're a socialist!

HILARY (*rises*). I think really I'm an anarchist.

CHARLES. That's quite an up and coming party, too, I believe.

HILARY. I don't know about that, but a lot of my friends won't allow their children to burn Guy Fawkes on a bonfire any more. (*Sits in sofa* R. *end.*)

CHARLES. Quite right. He was a romantic.

HILARY. Or maybe he was a realist.

CHARLES. Which are you?

HILARY. Me? I'm just a housewife. I suppose I'm a realist.

(CHARLES *shakes his head.*)
Why d'you shake your head?

CHARLES. Because I don't agree. Not from the evidence I have before me.

HILARY. What evidence d'you have before you?

CHARLES. Your eyes. Star witnesses you might call them.
HILARY. That's very prettily said. I thought you were going to be rude to me.
CHARLES. A rip-roaring grade A romantic. Do you often come up to London?
HILARY. About once a week.
CHARLES. Will you have lunch with me?
HILARY. No, thank you.
CHARLES. Why not?
HILARY. I have a sandwich at my hairdresser's.
CHARLES. What sort of sandwiches d'you like?
HILARY. Smoked salmon.
CHARLES. If I brought some to your hairdresser's could we have a picnic?
HILARY. No.
CHARLES. What do you do when you leave your hairdresser's?
HILARY. I drive home.
CHARLES. Have tea with me first.
HILARY. No.
CHARLES. Why not?
HILARY. I don't think I want to.
CHARLES. I don't think I believe you.
HILARY. You're very confident.
CHARLES. Courageous maybe, not confident.
            (HILARY *rises to fireplace.* CHARLES *also rises.*)
HILARY. By rights you should be in the West Corridor now, enjoying the "Portrait of a Burgomeister", by van Dyck. "Lady Rhyall and Children" by Nasmyth, *circa* 1800, unfinished. "Henrietta Maria, Wife of Charles the First", by Rawlinson, and a pair of mirrors by Robert Adam. Why don't you go and look at them?
CHARLES. I prefer looking at you.
HILARY. I'm not on exhibition.
CHARLES. Do you mind if I take your picture? (*He crosses above desk chair to get camera and back to face* HILARY.) The portrait of a lady of fashion, *circa* 1960, by Delacro.
HILARY. That's not fair. I've been packing mushrooms.
CHARLES (*he begins to prepare his camera, and takes a light meter from his pocket*). Or shall we call it just Hilary?
HILARY. I think "Subject unknown". (*Without waiting for her to consent, he takes a picture. He is quite evidently expert.*)

CHARLES (*after one picture*). You see, I shall want proof later on that the last twenty minutes really have happened. (*He puts camera back on desk.*) I may lie to myself and pretend they haven't. This picture will prove I'm wrong. That I really have seen you and talked to you. (*Returns to face* HILARY *below sofa.*)

HILARY. What d'you mean?

CHARLES. You know exactly what I mean.

HILARY. No, I don't.

CHARLES. They say the camera cannot lie. Nor can you, it seems. Not very well, anyway. Merely to avoid the truth is not good enough. Shall I say the truth out loud? So that you can deny it. Would that make you feel better? May I say it? May I whisper it?

HILARY. No—please no.

CHARLES. Why not? Are you frightened?

HILARY. Yes, I am.

CHARLES. Why, my darling?

HILARY. Don't call me that.

CHARLES. Because it's so sudden. Is that why?

HILARY. Not only that.

CHARLES. Would you have believed it could happen like this?

HILARY. I've heard of it.

CHARLES. I've heard of it, but I don't think I believed it.

HILARY. There ought to be some sort of warning, so that you can run away. There wasn't any.

CHARLES (*after a pause*). I've a confession to make. Why I came through that door, I mean. I'd been listening to you talking on the telephone.

HILARY. Eavesdropping!

CHARLES. No, listening to your voice. I thought it such a lovely voice, I opened the door. Then I saw you and you were lovely, too.

HILARY. Just a simple thing like a man coming through a door. And now look what's happened. It's like that game. He said to her. She said to him. And the consequences were.

CHARLES. What are the consequences?

HILARY. None.

CHARLES. I'm staying at Claridge's. Will you call me?

HILARY. No.

CHARLES. Please.

HILARY. No.

CHARLES. I shall stay in all the time in case you change your mind.

HILARY. I shan't.

SCENE I] THE GRASS IS GREENER 27

CHARLES. Women do sometimes. I shall hope. For two weeks I shall hope.
HILARY (*she puts her hand in her pocket, takes out a coin, and crosses to* CHARLES *below sofa*). Here's your half-crown back. Now go home to America. (*He takes half-crown with his* R. *hand, holding her* R. *wrist with his* L. *hand. He puts half-crown in* R. *pocket*.) And there's no fountain here for you to throw it in.
CHARLES. I shall keep it always.
HILARY. It's not the first time American money has been a nuisance in this country.
CHARLES. That's a little ungrateful, isn't it?
HILARY (*suddenly emotional*). I don't give a damn what it is.
   (CHARLES *takes her in his arms and kisses her. When the kiss ends they are both silent, and she is trembling. She breaks away from him and runs to* U.L. *door and opens it.*)
You must go. Go along the corridor until you come to the head of the staircase. At the bottom of the stairs turn right. That'll take you out to the car park.
   (CHARLES *gets hat and camera from desk, crosses above sofa table, turns in doorway to face* HILARY.)
CHARLES. Good-bye—Hilary.
HILARY (*too brightly*). It's been nice knowing you, Mr. Delacro.
CHARLES. Say good-bye nicely.
HILARY (*slowly*). Good-bye, Charles.
CHARLES. Good-bye—my love.
HILARY (*shaking her head as she looks at him*). I'm not your love.
CHARLES (*steps towards her*). Perhaps it's not good-bye either. (HILARY *steps back*.) Don't move. I want one more picture of you—as you are now. Don't move.
   (HILARY *is looking at him. He takes the photograph as* VICTOR *enters* R., *leaves door open, crossing above armchair from below sofa to bell above fireplace*.)
VICTOR. Darling, d'you know where my Bible is? Oh sorry, I thought you were alone.
HILARY (*down to above desk chair, hand on back of chair*). Isn't it by your bed?
VICTOR (*rings bell, then drops to* C. *of fireplace*). No. I wanted to read through the lessons before Sunday and I've searched high and low. It's really maddening. Perhaps Sellars knows where it is. (*Turning to* CHARLES.) You're from the Press, are you?

CHARLES. No. No, I'm not.
VICTOR. But you've got a camera. And you were taking a photograph.
HILARY. Mr. Delacro is an American.
VICTOR (*enlightened*). Oh, I see. I thought you were from "Good Housekeeping" or something.
HILARY. As you've probably already gathered, Mr. Delacro, this is my husband.
CHARLES (*drops round L. end of sofa to above* VICTOR *and holds out his hand*). I'm very happy to know you, sir.
VICTOR (*shaking hands*). How d'you do?
(*There is a slight pause as* VICTOR *looks at first one, then the other. He knows exactly what has happened.*)
It's quite absurd, isn't it? Two complete strangers meet—one pretends it's made him happy and the other replies by inquiring how he does.
HILARY (*making a brave effort*). I believe in Romany the gypsy greeting is "We have come to discuss the affairs of Egypt".
VICTOR. As Mr. Delacro is an American surely we can think of something less embarrassing than that.
CHARLES. What's wrong with "hulloa"?
VICTOR. What indeed? It's non-committal. Hulloa? (*Holds out his hand.*)
CHARLES (*shaking hands again*). Hulloa!
VICTOR. A little telephonic perhaps.
(*Enter* SELLARS *to just inside door.*)
SELLARS. You rang, milord?
VICTOR (*crossing to below sofa*). Oh yes, Sellars—I did. (*Turns to* CHARLES.) I must ring off now, I'm afraid. (*To above arm-chair.*) Have you seen my Bible anywhere, Sellars?
SELLARS. Oh dear, I'm more than sorry, milord—I really am. I'm afraid I've got it. I wanted to look something up.
VICTOR. First you borrow my "Times" and now you pinch my Bible. This is democracy running amok.
SELLARS. I'm very sorry indeed, milord. I'll put it back beside your bed. (*Turns to go.*)
VICTOR. Anyway you should have a Bible of your own.
SELLARS. The one you're using is mine, milord. (*Exit.*)
VICTOR (*laughing*). Now, why are we all standing about. (*To* CHARLES.) Do sit down. (HILARY *sits in desk chair.*) Tell me, are you a very keen photographer?
CHARLES (*sitting on stage end of chaise longue*). I get a lot of fun out of it.

VICTOR (*sits in armchair*). I bet you've got some beauties of the sentries outside Buckingham Palace.
CHARLES (*laughing*). As a matter of fact I have. In colour, too.
VICTOR. Was that one you took just now in colour?
CHARLES. Yes, it was.
VICTOR. You must let me have one if it comes out.
HILARY. Don't be so old fashioned, Victor. Nowadays all photographs "come out", as you call it. You're still living in the world of the Brownie.
VICTOR. Well, the last photograph I took was taken with a Brownie I've had since I was twelve, and that was published. I got ten and sixpence.
CHARLES. Is that so?
VICTOR. A couple of years ago. (*Rises and crosses below* HILARY *to below sofa.*) One of the Sunday picture papers published it. "The Field" turned it down. Never could understand why.
CHARLES. What was the subject?
VICTOR (*there is not a word of truth in any of this*). It was a grey squirrel with two heads and two tails. Most extraordinary sight. They're a fearful pest the grey squirrel but—d'you know?—I couldn't bring myself to shoot this one. Not after I'd taken its picture. Hilary here accused me of sentimentality, but there it was, I simply hadn't the heart.
HILARY. What on earth do you think you're talking about?
VICTOR. About that grey squirrel, darling.
HILARY. I've never heard of a grey squirrel with two heads and two tails in the whole of my life.
VICTOR. Yes, you have, darling. (*Up to* U.L. *door, and shuts it.*) Of course you have. We must try and keep this door shut. Anyone might come in. The autumn before last, you remember. (*Crossing above sofa table, picking up cigarette box to* L. *of* HILARY.) And when I let him go you said "Well, that's one squirrel that's proved two heads are better than one". And then I said "Well, it's heads he wins anyway".

(HILARY *gives* VICTOR *a withering look.*)
Are you over here for some time, Mr. Delacro? (*Crossing below sofa and offering empty cigarette box.*)
CHARLES. I'll be in Europe all summer, I hope.
VICTOR. Oh, I'm so sorry, there aren't any. (*Throws box on sofa and takes packet of ten from his pocket.*) Are you staying near here, or are

you making a quick tour of all the Stately Homes? There are four hundred of them now, half-a-crown ones, I mean.

CHARLES. Are there really?

VICTOR. Go on, I've got some more. (*Offering packet with one cigarette in it.*)

CHARLES. No, thank you, I don't smoke.

VICTOR. So that would take you the best part of the summer, wouldn't it? If you plan to see them all. (*Gives* HILARY *a quick look.*) Did you buy the booklet?

CHARLES. (*Takes it from his pocket.*) Yes I did.

VICTOR. Good. It's rather well done, don't you think?

HILARY. Mr. Delacro has just had a week's fishing and is on his way back to London.

VICTOR. Oh really—where've you been? (*Sits,* L. *end of sofa, putting cigarette box back on sofa table.*)

CHARLES. A friend of mine has a beat on the Hampshire Avon.

VICTOR. Whereabouts?

CHARLES. Fordingbridge. Quite near Salisbury.

VICTOR. Josh Peters?

CHARLES. That's right.

VICTOR. I've known Josh all my life. Since I was eight anyway. We had chicken-pox together.

HILARY. That must be a very wonderful bond between you.

VICTOR. How is he?

CHARLES. Very well. Put on a little weight since I saw him last maybe.

VICTOR. Took too much exercise when he was young. Well, you had good weather—how was the fishing?

CHARLES. On the whole very fair. A bit too much weed, and not enough cover on the banks yet. You couldn't really stalk a fish. But there were one or two big ones about. Josh did better than I did, I'm afraid.

VICTOR. So he damn well should; he knows that water as well as he knows his wife. Much prefers it, too.

HILARY. Don't be vulgar, Victor.

VICTOR. Perfectly true, my dear. And who could blame him? She stands six foot in her stocking feet, and there's always been a certain amount of doubt that she could read and write. You ought to have been there towards the end of the month when the mayfly hatch. Best couple of weeks of the whole season.

CHARLES. Josh did ask me, so maybe I will.
VICTOR. Very good article on the mayfly in last week's "Angling Times". Did you see it?
CHARLES. No, I didn't.
VICTOR. I'll get it for you. (*Rises, looking round room.*) Now where the hell is it? I suppose Sellars has got it. Look here, why don't you stay and have a cup of tea with us?
CHARLES. That's very kind of you.
VICTOR. Is there any of that Dundee cake left?
HILARY. I think so.
VICTOR. Then you must stay. It's simply delicious. D'you like Dundee cake?
CHARLES. Very much.
VICTOR. What could be better? Then after tea we'll take you round the gardens. (*Crosses to* D.R. *door.*) Now I'll get that "Angling Times" for you.
CHARLES. Don't bother.
VICTOR. It's no bother. I wonder if I can find the photograph of that squirrel—I'd like you to see it. You don't happen to know where it is, do you, darling? (*Exit.*)
    (*There is a silence.* CHARLES *watches* HILARY.)
HILARY. He's not always as facetious as that.
CHARLES (*rises to* C.). D'you reckon he knows what's happened?
HILARY. Oh yes, he knew; he knew at once.
CHARLES. That's my fault, I'm afraid. You can control yourself, but not the excitement inside you generating something into the atmosphere.
HILARY. No, not through you. Through me. (*Catching sight of the booklet he is still holding.*) Turn to the last page of that little booklet and read the last sentence.
CHARLES (*having found the place*). "The present Earl and Countess were married in nineteen forty-six. They have a son and heir Lord Wragley aged eleven, and a daughter, The Lady Emma Pooley, aged seven."
HILARY (*after a pause*). And we've been very happy.

CURTAIN

Scene 2

A week later. Afternoon.

The cuckoo is heard twice as curtain rises. VICTOR *enters reading "Henley", puts book on* R. *arm of sofa. The cuckoo is heard twice again. He crosses to desk, puts his hand on telephone receiver as if to lift it and decides not to. Crosses to bell, rings it. Crosses to drinks table, pours a whisky and water. The cuckoo is heard twice. He drops to front of fire with drink.*

SELLARS (*entering to just inside door*). You rang, milord?
VICTOR. Will you take those mushrooms to the station, Sellars? They're all packed.
    (SELLARS *shuts door and crosses to below* R. *end of sofa.*)
SELLARS. Yes, milord.
VICTOR. And tell Mrs. Bagshott if she ever gives me one to eat again, I'll sack her.
    (*Cuckoo.*)
SELLARS. Very good, milord.
VICTOR (*sniffing his fingers*). Damn things, I've just scrubbed my hands and I can still smell them. (*Crosses up round* L. *end of sofa.*)
SELLARS. I believe her Ladyship wears gloves, milord. (*Cuckoo.*) Will she be returning this evening? (*Having crossed to fireplace facing* U.S. *to* VICTOR.)
VICTOR (*crossing above sofa table*). I don't think so, Sellars. (*Cuckoo.*) I'll dine up here on a tray. (*By the window, listening.*) God, what a maddening bird that is. (*Drop to on stage of armchair.*)
SELLARS. It's a popular expression—isn't it?—milord—he's gone cuckoo.
VICTOR. Who's gone cuckoo?
    (*Cuckoo.*)
SELLARS. No one, milord. You said it was a maddening bird. I imagine that's how the expression originated. (*Above sofa to window.*) Shall I close the windows? That might muffle it a little.
VICTOR. That's admitting defeat. (*Cuckoo.*) No, thank you.
SELLARS (*down to level with* VICTOR *and* L. *of him*). His call always sounds like a sort of "*crie de coeur*" to me, milord.
VICTOR. Why's that?

SELLARS. Well, we all look forward so much to him, and he gets such a wonderful welcome when he first arrives—articles about him and letters in "The Times" and so on, and from then on everybody simply hates him. Having a failure after a good "press" must be very discouraging. Perhaps I'm looking at it more from the novelist's point of view, milord.
VICTOR. What's the time?

(SELLARS *lifts his glasses to look at his watch, puts them back, looks at the clock.*)

SELLARS. Nearly a quarter to six.
VICTOR. Then you'd better buck up.
SELLARS. Yes, milord. (*Crossing below* VICTOR.)
VICTOR (*puts his glass on drinks table*). Bring the evening papers from the station, will you?
SELLARS. Very good, milord. (*Exit* D.R.)

(VICTOR *goes out to put "Henley" away as* HATTIE *enters through the door leading to the public rooms. She is pretty, witty, gay, chic and sometimes a little outrageous. She puts her bag and scarf on chaise longue as* VICTOR *re-enters.*)

VICTOR (*to below arm-chair to on stage of it*). Hullo, Hattie. What are you doing here?
HATTIE (*crossing below sofa to* VICTOR). Hullo, darling. How are you? (*Kisses him on both cheeks.*)
VICTOR. Splendid, thanks. How are you?
HATTIE. Never better. Pleased to see me?
VICTOR. Not very.
HATTIE. Surprised to see me?
VICTOR. Not very.
HATTIE. Oh, and I paid half a crown to come in that way specially,
VICTOR. No, you didn't.
HATTIE. I call it a swindle. (*Cuckoo.*) What d'you mean, I didn't?
VICTOR. You came in that way because you knew a week ago today someone else came in that way, and you thought what fun it would be to do the same.

(HATTIE *crosses back below sofa to above chaise longue, takes hat off, puts it and gloves on the on-stage end of chaise longue.*)

HATTIE. Darling, I love you more and more every time I see you. But you're only half right. If I'd come in the normal way you might have told Sellars to say you'd gone out, or abroad or something.

(*Cuckoo.*) Such a pity. Our love for each other is founded on mutual distrust.

VICTOR (*laughing*). What leads you to suppose I love you?

HATTIE (*takes mirror from bag to check hair*). You did. Once upon a time. I think you even put it in writing.

VICTOR (*up to drinks table*). I suppose you'd like a drink?

HATTIE (*sits chair end of chaise longue and puts feet up on stool end*). I'd like some champagne, please.

VICTOR. I haven't any champagne. And I doubt very much if I'd give it you if I had.

HATTIE. I know how you must be feeling, darling, but you mustn't get bitter.

VICTOR (*leans on sofa table facing* HATTIE). Whisky or gin? (*Cuckoo.*) Or there's some cooking sherry in the kitchen.

HATTIE. Gin, please.

VICTOR. Tonic, soda, ginger ale or water?

HATTIE. Pink—and d'you mind burning the angostura, please?

VICTOR. I haven't any matches. (*Up to drinks table. He pours Angostura into glass.*)

HATTIE (*rises with bag to go round* R. *end of sofa. She finds matches and hands them to* VICTOR *above sofa table*). Here you are.

VICTOR (*looking at them*). Claridges. You been there recently?

HATTIE. Not recently, no.

VICTOR (*lights the drink*). I expect you got them from Hilary.

HATTIE. I expect I did.

VICTOR (*turns to get gin from drinks table*). Have you seen much of her?

HATTIE (*sits on stool below window, still holding bag*). Considering she's been staying with me, not very much—no. I had the other half of a grapefruit with her yesterday morning. I expect she'd have sent you her love, but she didn't know I was coming down. D'you know, it only took me an hour and twenty minutes, door to door?

VICTOR (*pours gin in glass*). On your broomstick.

HATTIE. She was looking very pretty but rather tired, I thought. I wondered if she needed a change.

VICTOR (*crossing to* L. *of* HATTIE *with jug of water*). How can people talk about progress? We used to burn women like you. Now we have to be content with Angostura. How much water?

HATTIE (*smiling sweetly*). Water, water, quench fire; thank you, darling. (*Rises, leaving bag by stool.*) You can see I'm making allowances for you, can't you?

VICTOR (*handing her glass*). Here you are.
HATTIE (*crosses down* R. *of sofa to below it*). Well, good luck! (*Raises her glass.*)
VICTOR (*drops to* R. *of sofa with his whisky*). You say that as though you think I'm going to need it.
HATTIE. Don't we all? You can't do anything without good luck. You need it from the moment you get out of bed in the morning to the moment you get back in again at night. (*With disgraceful immodesty.*) Particularly when you get back in again at night. (*Sits* L. *end of sofa.*)
VICTOR. You're a wanton.
HATTIE (*nodding*). Oh, but of course. (*Cuckoo.*) But I mean, you get out of bed in the morning and turn on your bath, then the telephone rings and you forget all about the bath and flood the flat below. It's going to cost me ninety pounds. If I'd had any luck, either the telephone wouldn't have rung or it might have been the day they clean the boiler, and there wouldn't have been any water coming out of the tap. Everything's luck, and you can't do a damn thing without it. Look at the lousy luck I had the day I introduced you to Hilary at Windsor races. Won the Tote Daily Double and lost you. And if you'd married me and not Hilary, then I wouldn't have married that horrid little man I did marry. Or spent all that money divorcing him. Wasn't much of a Tote Double either.
VICTOR. I suppose you blame me for that, too? (*Takes a drink.*)
HATTIE. I'm not blaming you for anything, darling. I was simply explaining how one always needs luck—even with bath water.
VICTOR. Why've you come down here?
HATTIE. Two reasons.
VICTOR. What are they?
HATTIE. Firstly, I'm very fond of Hilary.
VICTOR. And secondly?
HATTIE (*moves up to* R. *end of sofa*). I'm very fond of you.
VICTOR. So what?
HATTIE. I thought you might need cheering up, my sweet.
VICTOR. Now, Hattie, be honest. What was the real reason?
HATTIE. I do hate it when people say "be honest". It puts one at such a disadvantage. And you must know as well as I do—that saying it to me is sheer waste of breath.
VICTOR. It was curiosity, wasn't it? You wanted to see how I'd reacted to my wife falling in love with another man.

HATTIE. He's not "just another man", darling, he's a millionaire.
VICTOR (*ignoring this*). Well, I'll tell you how I've reacted. I'm very annoyed. (*Crosses to armchair.*) Very annoyed, very miserable, very at a loss, and very lonely. (*Sits armchair.*)
HATTIE. And very jealous?
VICTOR. And very jealous. I don't like seeing that look on her face except when she's looking at me. But she wasn't looking at me, she was looking at him. That was on Friday. All day Saturday and Sunday I waited for her to say she was going to London for a few days, and on Monday morning she did. A very depressing and rather jumpy week-end.
HATTIE. Did you try to stop her?
VICTOR. I looked up a train for her, helped her pack, and drove her to the station.
HATTIE. Yes, she told me. Why didn't you try to stop her?
VICTOR. Because I'm not a fool.
HATTIE. I must confess I've never thought you were until now. (*Rises with glass to* D.C. *facing* VICTOR.) Wouldn't it have been safer if she hadn't seen him again?
VICTOR. From my point of view it was essential that she did see him again. If she hadn't I should have been the obstacle preventing her from seeing him. That would have damaged our relationship; even at the risk of encouraging theirs, that's the last thing I want to do. Anyway, I doubt if I could have stopped her.
HATTIE. I don't want to be a wet blanket, darling, but isn't your relationship damaged already?
VICTOR. I hope not permanently, and not necessarily beyond repair. It all depends.
HATTIE. On what?
VICTOR. On me, on Hilary. And Mr. Delacro.
HATTIE. That name is going to crop up a lot in the conversation. Don't you think we ought to call him Charles?
VICTOR. Is that usual?
HATTIE. Oh, nowadays surely it must be.
VICTOR. Have you met him?
HATTIE. I haven't met an unmarried millionaire for years. I'd be so over excited if I did. I'd probably curtsey. (*She curtseys right down to the ground and stays there.*)
VICTOR. Did Hilary talk to you about him?
HATTIE. All the time—except when she talked about you.

VICTOR. What did she say?
HATTIE. She said she loved you.
VICTOR. And was in love with him.
HATTIE. Mad about him.
VICTOR. There's a difference, isn't there? (*Furiously.*) I've always known no good would come of my opening this house to the public. Has she been with him all the time?
HATTIE. I imagine so. (*Rises, crosses to on stage of chaise longue.*) They went to Kew Gardens yesterday on a bus. I thought that was rather a bad sign.
VICTOR. Now what?
HATTIE. From what she said, they kiss good-bye and she comes home tomorrow.
VICTOR. And what am I supposed to do?
HATTIE. Thank your lucky stars.
VICTOR. That she's coming back?
HATTIE. Yes.
VICTOR. You think there was ever a danger she might not have come back?
HATTIE (*shrugs her shoulders*). Not really, I suppose, but you must admit that Charles is obviously competition; and of course he's doing his damnedest.
VICTOR. I'm sure he is.
HATTIE. And as I said before, she's simply mad about him.
VICTOR. So I saw for myself. And he's doing his best to persuade her to leave me and marry him?
HATTIE (*crosses to* R. *of sofa and sits on* R. *arm facing audience*). Oh yes, so I gathered.

(VICTOR *rises and goes round* R. *end of sofa. He puts glass on sofa table, and goes on round* L. *end of sofa to below it.*)

VICTOR. No time wasted, eh? The caféteria system. See something you want, put it on a tray and take it away with you. It's quite astonishing, isn't it? Here's a man. A reasonable, decent sort of man, who'd no more dream of pinching my cuff links than he would of poaching my salmon. Yet he'll pay half a crown at the gate, walk into my house, and without disturbing his conscience in any way, calmly endeavour to steal my wife.
HATTIE. By the same token Hilary wouldn't cheat at cards. There's no honour where there's sex, I'm happy to say. (*Holding out her*

glass which VICTOR *takes.*) If you'll give me some gin, I'll give you some advice. I don't believe in something for nothing.

VICTOR. D'you want all that bonfire business again?

HATTIE. Yes, please.

VICTOR. What a nuisance you are. (*Crosses by* L. *end of sofa to drinks table and begins the laborious business with a clean glass.*) Well go on—go on—go on. Advise me.

HATTIE. Like most men who've had success with women, you flatter yourself you understand them. (*Crosses to desk chair which is facing* U.S.) Don't be a mug, my sweet. (*Cuckoo.*) You haven't a clue. (*Cuckoo.*) Hilary's paramount emotion at the— (*Sits, leaning over back of chair.*) I say what a lovely word "paramount"—I don't think I've ever used it before. Hilary's paramount emotion at the moment is neither her passion for Charles nor her love for you, it's a feeling of complete bewilderment (*Cuckoo.*) that her values, her standards, her whole existence can be knocked cock-eyed in half an hour. When she comes home just remember that. And forget everything else.

VICTOR. And clap hands and jump for joy. (*Hands* HATTIE *her drink, then breaks up to window and looks out.*)

HATTIE. If you want her back, that's the way to play it.

(*The cuckoo has been calling again.*)

That bird is a little too emphatic, isn't he? What did Shakespeare say? "A cuckoo then on every tree, mocks married men." (*Cuckoo.*)

VICTOR (*down by* R. *end of sofa to below it*). Supposing I can't play it that way?

HATTIE. Because of your pride?

VICTOR (*wanders to fireplace*). Well, what's wrong with pride?

HATTIE. It comes before a fall, they say.

VICTOR (*wanders back to below* L. *end of sofa*). Nonsense, it's a very good thing. Been a great help to me all my life.

HATTIE. How?

VICTOR. Oh, not crying on Victoria platform.

HATTIE. You're going back a bit, aren't you?

VICTOR. Well—being jolly when you lose, being hearty at the dentist. Anyway it's nothing to do with pride. It's because I love her. I've loved her for thirteen years, and each one of them I've loved her more.

HATTIE. Have you been faithful to her all those years?

(*Cuckoo.*)

VICTOR. Yes, I have. (*Catching her eye and realizing the hopelessness of denial.*) Well, that's beside the point. (*Crosses below sofa to fireplace.*)
HATTIE (*kneels in chair facing* VICTOR). It's not beside the point, it is the point. A sharpish one, too. What's sauce for the goose. Remember?
VICTOR (*loudly*). Rubbish! (*Comes below* C. *of sofa.*) The whole fundamental difference between men and women is that what's sauce for the goose is not sauce for the gander—that's why women wear wedding rings and men don't. (*Drops to above chaise longue, moves hat, scarf and gloves to chair end.*)
HATTIE. First proud, now arrogant.
VICTOR (*sits on stage end of chaise longue*). Well, it's true!
HATTIE (*as if to a child*). Silly, headstrong boy.
VICTOR. Anyway the fact remains—the solemn fact remains, that my world goes round only because of her. She's the focus point of my whole existence. Everything I've done or accomplished, which doesn't amount to much I dare say, has either been for her or on account of her. We've been friends as well as lovers. And if I sing in my bath it's because I'm going to have breakfast with her. Without her I don't say I'd be lost, but I certainly wouldn't be very clear in my mind quite which way to turn.
HATTIE (*rises and leaves glass on desk, crosses below sofa, kneeling and facing* VICTOR). Tell her all that. Talk the whole thing over.
VICTOR. Fatal. The spoken word—like the sped arrow and the lost opportunity—it doesn't come back. When a situation like this is admitted out loud it means it's accepted. If it's accepted it's got to be discussed. And each time you discuss it you get farther apart, until in the end you're so far away from each other you have to shout, and once you start shouting the whole thing becomes hopeless. She knows that as well as I do.
HATTIE. Then do as I say, just be gentle and kind and understanding.
VICTOR. Like a husband treats his bride on the honeymoon? She's not my bride, she's my wife! And it's all too apparent this isn't our honeymoon. No, what I've got to do is to get Mr. Bloody Delacro out of her heart, out of her mind, and out of the God damned country.

(*Cuckoo.*)

HATTIE. And how d'you propose to do that?
VICTOR. I don't know, I wish I did. All I know is, that she'll turn up here tomorrow as brave as a lion, as bright as a button, with her suitcase in one hand and her sacrifice in the other—and she'll be

coming back, not because of me, but because of the children. Well, as far as I'm concerned, that's the wrong reason. I want her back simply and solely because of me.

HATTIE. Or not at all?

VICTOR. I think probably yes. Or not at all.

HATTIE (*rises and sits* R. *end of sofa*) That's selfish and short-sighted and very stupid.

VICTOR. Selfish maybe. Not the other two. I know my limitations, I couldn't live with Hilary watching her longing for somebody else. (*Rises and faces fire.*) Forty-eight hours of that last week-end was enough, thank you. I couldn't face the humiliation of the dressing-room. I couldn't stand a polite, patched up, second best, forlorn sort of life, patiently waiting the dawn of indifference. Not for me, Hattie, thank you very much, not for me. The role of forgiving husband is always a difficult one in triangular dramas. I should find it utterly beyond me. Far better not to attempt it. Anyway there's another possibility.

HATTIE. What's that?

VICTOR. That she'd fail. She might come back here, eat her heart out for a while and then run off. The well known little note, that she couldn't stand it any longer—and an air line ticket to Romantic Places and Mr. Delacro. There's no guarantee that wouldn't happen.

HATTIE. Then you'd marry me at last and we'd live happily ever after.

VICTOR. No, if I'm going to preserve our marriage, and I don't mean a patched-up bargain for the sake of the children, then something's got to be done—and done immediately.

HATTIE. If Hilary's prepared to make a sacrifice for the children then I think you should, too.

VICTOR (*at* L. *end of sofa*). It's not that I wouldn't, it's quite simply that I couldn't. The only way to make a sacrifice is to enjoy it enormously. Wallow and slosh about it in. I'm not the type. I should bungle it hopelessly.

HATTIE. You may encounter opposition. Hilary may not like having her sacrifice flung back in her teeth.

VICTOR. How d'you mean?

HATTIE. She seemed to me pretty determined on coming home and continuing to be the good little wife and perfect mother.

VICTOR. With the aching heart? (*Starts to straighten the sleeve of his jersey.*)

HATTIE. Yes, but he's given her a mink coat, which should stop the ache a bit.
VICTOR. He's done what? (*He is made motionless by this remark.*)
HATTIE. He's given her a mink coat.
VICTOR. Has he, by God! (*After a pause he crosses below sofa to on-stage of armchair.*) Well damn him and blast him, and I hope he rots in hell.
HATTIE. A wild mink. An absolute beauty.
VICTOR (*crossing to* R. *end of sofa*). And how is the good little wife and the perfect mother going to explain that away?
HATTIE. Poor sweet, she was rather worried about it. (*Very cheerfully.*) But I expect she'll think of something.
VICTOR (*quietly*). I've been wanting to give her a mink ever since we were married, and next Christmas I could just about have done it. I've a damn good mind to shoot him.
HATTIE. I think we should try and avoid bloodshed, darling.
VICTOR. Give me one good reason why.
HATTIE. It's a little old fashioned.
VICTOR. Then it's high time it was brought up to date. I don't like the ways of the modern world, and in particular the ways of the New World where Mr. Delacro comes from. If a man takes a fancy to a married woman, he gives her a mink coat and expects the husband to give her a divorce, which is just about as quick and no harder to get than a cup of instant coffee.
HATTIE. We have that sort of thing over here as well, you know.
VICTOR (*moving to telephone*). Of course we do. We have Coca Cola, too, and where did it come from? (*Crosses up to above desk and picks up telephone.*) How damn well dare she imagine she can come back here flaunting a mink coat in my face, and pretending she's paid for it out of money she's won off Littlewoods? My God, she's got a gall.
HATTIE. Well, you couldn't expect her not to take it, could you, darling? Not wild mink. Now could you—I mean apart from it being insured for three thousand pounds?
VICTOR. Three thousand pounds!
HATTIE. Three thousand pounds. I expect it's got a sentimental value as well.
VICTOR. Mayfair 8860 please.
HATTIE. That's Claridge's number.
VICTOR (*his manner and mood entirely changed*). Easy one to remember, isn't it?

HATTIE (*rises*). What are you going to do?
VICTOR. I'm going to talk to Mr. Delacro if he's there, if not I shall leave a message.
HATTIE (*round to* R. *end of sofa*). What sort of message?
VICTOR (*after consideration*). An invitation. (*He waits a moment or two.*) Hullo. Claridge's? I want to speak to Mr. Delacro, please—Mr. Charles Delacro. This is Tommy Steele here. Thanks a lot, baby. (*His hand over the mouthpiece.*) It's the only way to get any service from telephone girls. I used to be Dickie Valentine. I switched to Tommy Steele about eighteen months ago. Hullo? Is that Charles Delacro? (HATTIE *crosses below desk up* R. *side of it and sits, on edge,* R. *of him.*) It's a Victor Rhyall here. How are you? Good.
    (HATTIE *crosses to him and puts her ear to the receiver.*)
VICTOR. Listen, I must apologize for not giving you more notice, but we wondered if you weren't doing anything better you'd care to come down for the week-end. (HATTIE *pulls telephone away from* VICTOR'S *ear.*)
HATTIE. You're out of your mind.
VICTOR (*his hand over the mouthpiece*). Shut up and go and sit down.
    (HATTIE *goes round behind him to* L. *of him.*)
Oh splendid. What a bit of luck. It'll be very quiet, I'm afraid. Just ourselves, and possibly a rather boring friend of Hilary's who drinks gin all day.
    (HATTIE *pinches his behind hard.*)
Ouch! What? No, no, a little interference, that's all. (HATTIE *pulls window stool down to* L. *of* VICTOR *and stands on it.*) Bring a rod and we'll frighten some fish. Any time after lunch. Splendid. Look forward to seeing you. Half a minute, I've just thought of something. My wife's coming down tomorrow. Yes, she's been in London all the week. I wonder if you'd be very kind and give her a lift? That is good of you. May I tell her to get in touch with you at Claridge's? Till tomorrow. Good-bye. (*Puts down the receiver and rubs his behind.*) You hurt me just then.
HATTIE. You shouldn't say I was boring. I think you're barking mad and I bet he doesn't come.
VICTOR (*drops down* R. *of sofa, then below it*). I'm not barking mad, and of course he'll come. Gives him another forty-eight hours with her. And he's saying to himself "Anything can happen in forty-eight hours". He thought of that before he accepted.
    (*Cuckoo.*)

HATTIE. Was Hilary with him, d'you think?
VICTOR. Probably.
HATTIE. And heard him accept?
VICTOR. Obviously.
  (HATTIE *gets off stool, picks up bag, crossing in front of* VICTOR *to above chaise longue.*)
HATTIE. Then I expect Charles had his behind pinched, too. She's not going to like it, you know.
VICTOR. She's going to hate it like hell and be as jumpy as all get out, but unless she's prepared to admit the whole thing, there's absolutely nothing she can do about it. And if she does admit the whole thing, being a well brought up girl, she'll realize she's got to return the mink.
HATTIE. Perhaps you do understand a little about women after all. I take it I'm invited, too?
VICTOR. Of course. I shall need your support. Did you bring a bag?
HATTIE. When you address me I prefer the word suitcase, but as a matter of fact I did. It's in the car outside. But that doesn't mean I'm staying. (*Comes* C.) I'm jumpy, too!
VICTOR. Of course you're staying; it's your duty to stay.
HATTIE (*sits* L. *end of sofa*). Well if you say it's my duty, darling, I suppose I must. By the way, I told Hilary I was going to the Crockfords for the week-end.
VICTOR (*sits* R. *end of sofa*). I'll say you've changed your mind as it's going to be more fun here.
HATTIE. Machiavelli might think it fun. I think it's going to be torture, but as you insist it's my duty I suppose I've got to put up with it. I wonder what is the exact interpretation of above and beyond the call of duty.
VICTOR. Hattie, it's just a nice quiet English week-end, that's all. You'll enjoy it.
HATTIE. I'd enjoy it more if I knew what you were up to. You've thought up something horrible, I know that much.
VICTOR. Nonsense. Let's say I shall exploit any given opportunities.
HATTIE. Now what are you going to do with me until the others arrive—play scrabble?
VICTOR (*genially*). You can't spell—can you?—but if that's what you'd like.
HATTIE. No, it's not. I'd like a good dinner and a bottle of something very expensive and preferably fizzy.

VICTOR. Then I'll take you over to "The Horse and Groom". It's not far and not bad.

HATTIE (*being wicked*). How delicious! (*Leans her head on his shoulder.*) I shall enjoy having a gorgeous dinner with you again, darling. Will there be lovely soft lighting, d'you think?

VICTOR. If there were any danger of that I'd take a torch. (*Rises to* R. *end of sofa.*) You're not to be outrageous, Hattie.

(*The cuckoo starts to sing again.*)

There's that damned bird again.

(*With sudden fury he slams the window shut.*)

HATTIE (*brightly*). Cuckoo, cuckoo. (*Rises to above chaise longue and takes handkerchief from her bag.*) D'you know? I've a feeling it's flown here straight from Claridge's.

CURTAIN

ACT TWO

Scene 1

The following evening.
The window curtains are not yet drawn though outside the twilight has turned to nightfall. The bracket lamps on the mantelpiece, the D.L. *tablelamp and the lamp* L. *of the windows are on. A fire has been lit and an unfinished game of "Scrabble" is spread out on a low coffee table.*

    HILARY *is standing above the fireplace and* HATTIE *is sitting on stool end of chaise longue with her back to the audience.*

    The sofa is now facing the fire and this stool is in front of the sofa.

HILARY (*to above sofa table, looking at* D.R. *door*). What on earth d'you imagine they're talking about?
HATTIE. Fish.
    (HILARY *crosses down between fire and stool. She sits on chair chaise longue which has been turned slightly up stage.*)
HILARY. Oh, not still!
HATTIE. From a woman's point of view, the amount of time men spend talking about fish is quite humiliating, but perhaps on this occasion we ought to be rather thankful.
HILARY. I'm sure we shouldn't have left them alone together.
HATTIE. Nonsense, darling. They are behaving like positive buddies.
HILARY. I don't trust Victor when he's genial.
HATTIE. I don't trust him—period. Has he said anything? (*She takes a peppermint from a box which is on the floor* D.S. *of stool, hands it to* HILARY *and takes one herself.*)
HILARY. About Charles? Not a word. I've only seen him alone for about five minutes when we were dressing for dinner, then he sang all the time "Thanks for the memory" until I could have screamed.
HATTIE (*amused*). He is a brute, isn't he?
HILARY (*rises, crosses below sofa to* R. *of it*). What's he up to? Why's he being so infuriating? What's his object?
HATTIE. Perhaps he hasn't any object.
HILARY. Oh, nonsense. He must have some reason. He hasn't organized this ghastly situation for nothing. (*Sits on back of sofa.*)

HATTIE. Maybe he's a sadist. And enjoys watching you and Charles suffering. On the other hand, of course, he might be the other thing.
HILARY. What other thing?
HATTIE. You know, just the opposite. A what-you-may-call-'em. Someone who gets a kick out of being made unhappy. (*Crosses sofa, kneeling and leaning over the back of it* D.S. *of* HILARY.) What's he called? Begins with an M.
HILARY. Masochist.
HATTIE. That's the chap.
HILARY. Rubbish!
HATTIE. I couldn't agree more. Seems to me absolute rubbish but there it is. And it's quite well known, or so I read in my Sunday papers. They say it's a result of a public school education.
HILARY (*rises to on-stage of armchair*). Oh, shut up, darling, you've got the whole thing muddled.
HATTIE. Have I? Well, I don't wonder. It is muddling, isn't it? It is to me, anyway. I'm just a girl—
HILARY. Who can't say no. (*Turns to face* HATTIE.) Which reminds me—what did you and Victor do last night?
HATTIE. I told you, darling. We had a delicious dinner at the "Horse and Groom" and then came back here and played "Scrabble".
HILARY. I never quite trust you with Victor. Why didn't you dine here?
HATTIE. Victor said he felt like going out.
HILARY. Oh, he did! (*Crosses below sofa to fireplace and throws peppermint paper in fire.*) What time did you go to bed?
HATTIE. About half-past twelve, I think.
HILARY. Did Victor have much to drink?
HATTIE. Very little as far as I remember.
(HILARY *turns to look at* HATTIE.)
HILARY. But you can't play "Scrabble"—not with grown-up people. (*Sits on chair chaise longue.*)
HATTIE. I know how to cheat at it. (*Sweetly.*) Where did you dine, darling?
HILARY (*a little discomfited*). The White Tower.
HATTIE. Oh, how gorgeous. And what time did you go to bed—nice and early? (HILARY *rises and faces fire.*) That was a splendid one of Victor's, wasn't it? (*Sits on stool looking at "Scrabble".*)
HILARY. What was?
HATTIE. His last turn before dinner. When you'd just got "conduct"

and he put "mis" in front of it. That put us in the lead, I think—where's the score? (*Back on to sofa looking for the score in the cushions.*)
HILARY (*turning and kicking viciously at the board, upsetting it and all the letters on the floor*). Damn boring game.
HATTIE. Yes, darling, madly boring, I quite agree. (*She goes on hands and knees between sofa and stool facing audience, takes the box from under the stool and starts to put pieces in it.*) We'll say Sellars knocked it over putting down the coffee tray. Come on, give me a hand.

(HILARY *goes on hands and knees between stool and fire facing audience and starts picking up pieces that side.* [*Letters have been planted under each side of the sofa and under chair chaise longue.*])

I think it was simply wonderful of you not to kick it all over the room when he actually did it. Tremendous self-control it must have been. I was really filled with admiration.
HILARY. Is that why you giggled?

(HATTIE *crawls across in front of stool to get pieces from under chair chaise longue, then crawls backwards into* HILARY's *original position.* HILARY *crawls round behind stool.*)

HATTIE. That was pure hysteria. You must admit it was quite a moment. I didn't dare to look at Charles.

(*Enter* SELLARS D.R. *with the coffee tray, shutting the door. They are both hidden from his immediate view. He stands looking round the room rather puzzled.*)

What are we going to do for the rest of the evening?
HILARY (*looking under sofa*). Don't ask me.
HATTIE. Unless there's a panel of bachelors discussing marriage and divorce, perhaps it would be less embarrassing to watch television.

(SELLARS *reacts to* HATTIE's *voice. He moves further into the room until he sees them both on the floor.*)

SELLARS (*relieved*). Ah, there you are! (*Coming to back of sofa* HILARY *kneels up on hearing his voice.*) I beg your pardon, milady! I couldn't understand where the voices were coming from.
HILARY. Put the coffee on here, will you? (*Clearing all the bits left on the stool into the box on the floor.*)
SELLARS (*goes round above sofa and puts tray on stool*). Yes, milady. Let me help you pick up these pieces, milady.
HILARY. I think we've got them all now. Unless there are any under the sofa. (*Indicating the* R. *side of sofa.*)

(SELLARS *goes on hands and knees* R. *of sofa and finds two letters.*

He hands them to HILARY *round* D.S. *end of sofa. Now they are all three on their knees facing audience,* HILARY *in the* C.)

Thank you, Sellars. What are you laughing at?

SELLARS. I'm sorry, milady. I really couldn't help it. We must look as though we're playing bears.

HATTIE. Who's been eating my porridge?

HILARY. And who's been sleeping in my bed?

(HATTIE's *laughter ceases abruptly.* HILARY *rises to above fireplace.* SELLARS *crawls to* U.S. *end of sofa.*

HATTIE *starts to collect the "Scrabble" box and board together.*)

Would you draw the curtains, please?

SELLARS. Certainly, milady. (*Rises, unhooks curtains* R. *end then* L. *end. There is a silence while he does this.*)

HILARY. And put another log on the fire. (*Draws curtains.*) That makes it more cosy, doesn't it, darling?

(HATTIE *rises with all the "Scrabble" things and crosses in front. She puts them on the desk.* HILARY *sits on chair of chaise longue.*)

HATTIE. Just about as cosy as when you fasten your safety-belt.

SELLARS (*having put a log on the fire comes above sofa table*). Will that be all, milady?

HILARY. Yes, thank you, Sellars. You might look into the dining-room and tell them coffee'll be ready in five minutes.

SELLARS. Very good, milady. (*Round sofa to* R. *of it.*)

HILARY. Oh, and did you notice a rather shabby old suitcase in Mr. Delacro's car?

SELLARS. I put it in his room.

HILARY. No, that one's mine.

SELLARS. I'll change it over. Have you a key for it?

HILARY. No, I haven't, but don't worry about that, just put it in my room. (*She puts coffee pot on floor* D.S. *of fireplace and plugs it into the switch.*)

SELLARS. Very good, milady.

(SELLARS *crosses in front of* HATTIE *who is putting on her jacket which has been set over back of desk chair. He switches on* D.R. *lamp then crosses to door, opens it, then switches on chandelier from switch below* D.R. *door and then goes out* D.R.)

(*There is a pause.*)

HATTIE (*below desk chair*). I'm sorry I was bitchy just now.

HILARY. It was my fault. I'm sorry, too. (*Pause.*) Oh, Hattie, what a hell of a thing to happen, isn't it?

HATTIE. Yes, darling. I suppose sometime tomorrow you want me to take Victor for a long walk so you can see Charles alone.
HILARY. Yes, please.
HATTIE. To say good-bye or *au revoir?*
HILARY. I don't know. I honestly don't know. It's a dreadful thing to confess, but I honestly do not know. I can give no guarantee of what I'm going to do or how I'm going to behave. D'you find that shocking?
HATTIE. Coming from you, I do rather. Well, surprising anyhow. Of course, it's the sort of feeling I've been having ever since I was about eleven. (*Crosses to sofa and sits on the back of it.*)
HILARY. I could have said good-bye to him last night. I think I could. I'd made up my mind and I was all prepared. But now Victor's done everything he can think of to make it more difficult. I thought at least he might have been understanding—not sympathetic even—just understanding. But not a bit of it. He doesn't seem to give a damn about me. (*Rises to face fire.*) He knows darned well I couldn't live without the children, and he thinks he's got me, so he's sitting down there being charming and polite like a beastly little boy who's asked his friend to tea.
HATTIE. Darling, the point is he's asked your friend to tea. Now what's he done that for? That's what I'd like to know.
HILARY. Did he talk about Charles to you last night?
HATTIE. Oh yes, of course he did. He was rather rude about him.
HILARY. What did he say?
HATTIE. He said, in order to commemorate the number of liberties Americans had taken in this country in the last fifteen years—it was high time England had a Statue of Liberty of her own. Or did he say Libertine? I can't remember,
HILARY (*crossing to above sofa table*). Dreary pompous little Englishman.
HATTIE. Grosvenor Square would be the proper site, he said.
HILARY (*on round sofa to between it and armchair*). What else did he say? He must have said something else. Isn't he upset?
HATTIE. Yes, I think he's upset. I asked him if he thought there was any possibility of your running away with Charles.
HILARY (*just on stage of armchair*). And what did he say?
HATTIE. He said he thought it would be a pity.
HILARY (*furious*). A pity! What's he mean, a pity?
HATTIE. But that if you did he wouldn't accept responsibility for either the mushrooms or Miss Mathews.

HILARY. And that was all?

HATTIE. Yes—except every time he heard the cuckoo he lost his temper. But on the whole he seemed to be taking it quite remarkably well.

HILARY. Doesn't he think of me at all? Doesn't he realize what I'm sacrificing! That if I give up Charles it's going to break my heart.

HATTIE. Hearts mend, Hil darling. They mend as good as new. They're designed for that particular purpose. (*Rises and crosses to* L. *of* HILARY.) Now quick, before they come up, tell me what you've done about the mink. You can't possibly give that up. That'd be a heartbreak you could never mend. Where is it?

HILARY. It's here. You didn't breathe a word about that to Victor, did you?

HATTIE. My dear, what d'you take me for? It's here, is it?

HILARY. I brought it down.

HATTIE. But what are you going to say?

HILARY. Well, I've had rather a brain wave. (*Hears voices outside, so changes the subject.*)

    (VICTOR *opens* D.R. *door,* CHARLES *enters to below armchair.*
    HILARY *crosses below sofa and sits on chair chaise longue.*
    VICTOR *shuts door, enters to* R. *of sofa;* HATTIE *sits on back of sofa.*)

So I went to Harrods and bought a sponge.

VICTOR (*his manner throughout the following scene is casual and charming, never bright or forced*). There was an old boy who used to dine here in my youth who, when we joined the ladies, always entered the drawing-room with the words "Better is a dinner of herbs where love is, than a stalled ox and hatred therewith". My mother was always furious. But I so agree, don't you? Better a dinner of herbs where love is. Hattie, a glass of kümmel—or did you finish the bottle after lunch? (*Up to drinks table.*)

HATTIE (*rises up to drinks table* R. *of* VICTOR). Now, don't you talk like that. You were so jolly mean with it I decided I'd give you some bigger glasses. Have you been talking about fish?

    (HILARY *having unplugged coffee pot, crosses and sits on sofa and starts to pour out coffee.*)

CHARLES (*up to on stage of desk chair*). No, we were talking about women.

HATTIE. Fancy that!

CHARLES. Or rather ballerinas, which perhaps isn't quite the same thing, Mrs. Urquhart.

HATTIE. Will you do me a great favour?
CHARLES (*leaning on back of desk chair*). Why certainly.
HATTIE. Never call me by that name.
CHARLES. Why not?
HATTIE. Eueugh!
VICTOR (*handing glass to* HATTIE). There you are, Mrs. Urquhart darling, the unexpended portion of a day's ration. (HATTIE *takes glass, crosses to fireplace, puts glass on mantelpiece.*) Hilary, what for you? Similar, as they say in saloon bars?
HILARY. Well, you haven't got anything else, have you?
VICTOR. Sssh, darling, please. Not in front of a millionaire. And as a matter of fact I've some very good brandy, but I'm keeping that. For Charles and myself.
HILARY. I thought you were going to say for Christmas. I'll have some brandy, please.
VICTOR (*smiling*). And the stalled ox and hatred therewith! Charles, brandy?
CHARLES. Thank you.
HILARY (*handing coffee to* HATTIE). Here's your coffee, darling.
VICTOR (*at the drink table, his back to* HILARY). Thank you, darling.
HILARY. Not you.
VICTOR. Oh, I beg your pardon, I thought you said "darling". (*Turns to drinks table.*)

(HATTIE *sits chair chaise longue.*)

HILARY. So I did. Here's yours. (*She hands cup over back of sofa to* CHARLES.)
VICTOR (*turning from drinks table*). Thank you, darling. Oh, it's really too confusing. Next time I shall bring my own. (*Turns again to drinks table.*)
HILARY. Victor.
VICTOR. Yes, darling?
HILARY. Here's your coffee.

(VICTOR *drops to above the stool, gives* CHARLES *his brandy, takes his coffee, gives* HILARY *her brandy.*

CHARLES *crosses above* VICTOR *to fireplace, puts brandy on mantelpiece.*)

VICTOR. Thank you, darling. Nihil dictum quod non dictum prius.
HATTIE. What's that mean?
VICTOR. Nothing is said that hasn't been said before. I'd said "thank you, darling" three times.

HATTIE. Oh, how dull. In medical books they always use Latin for the interesting bits.

HILARY. Hattie!

HATTIE. Well, they do, darling. Don't you remember in the one I borrowed from you it was all—

VICTOR (*up to drinks table, taking coffee with him*). Very frustrating for you.

CHARLES. Are we going to finish our "Scrabble"?

HILARY. I'm awfully sorry, but I'm afraid Sellars knocked the whole thing over when he brought in the coffee.

VICTOR (*pouring out his brandy*). Thank you, darling.

HILARY. What are you thanking me for?

VICTOR (*puts his brandy on sofa table*). It's just habit. Every time you say coffee, I say thank you, darling.

CHARLES. Now isn't that just too bad. During dinner I thought of a way to use my Zee—sorry, Zed to you.

HATTIE. Was that when Victor was talking about the future of the Liberal Party or Burgos Cathedral?

CHARLES. Now don't embarrass me. (*Puts coffee cup on mantelpiece and sees two scrabble letters in hearth.*)

HATTIE. I didn't listen to a word he said, either.

(VICTOR *drops to behind sofa, having left brandy on sofa table.*)

CHARLES (*stopping to pick something up*). Here are two more scrabble letters. (*Looking at them.*) O and K. O.K.! Well, that must be a good omen.

HILARY. Yes, it must be, mustn't it?

VICTOR (*behind* C. *of sofa*). Try them round the other way.

CHARLES. K.O.

VICTOR. Quite different, isn't it?

CHARLES. Knocked out. Well, that could be an omen, too, I guess.

VICTOR. You never can tell, can you?

CHARLES. Which way round things are going to happen?

VICTOR. Or what to put first and what place second. If we knew that we'd all be a lot happier. Don't you agree?

CHARLES (*smiling and quite at ease*). Oh yes, but as a general rule I'd say put yourself first and the other fellow second.

VICTOR. And supposing the other fellow disputes your arrangement?

CHARLES. Then you enter into competition.

VICTOR. And the race is to the swift, and the battle to the strong?

CHARLES. Sure.

VICTOR. D'you know, I'm not at all sure? (*Breaks* R. *a little.*) In theory I have to disagree with you; in practice you may well be right. It's a little primitive, but what's wrong with that?
HATTIE. What's primitive?
VICTOR. You are, darling.
HATTIE (*delighted*). Oh, am I really? Or is he being insulting? (*Puts her coffee cup on tray.*)
CHARLES (*puts his coffee cup down to hand* HATTIE *her kümmel from mantelpiece, then picks up his brandy*). On the contrary, I'd say he paid you a compliment.
VICTOR (*round above sofa to hand his coffee cup to* HILARY). He just says that because he is, too.
HATTIE. Is Hilary primitive?
VICTOR. I'm beginning to wonder.
HATTIE. And what are you?
VICTOR. Sellars told me the other day that I was traditional. (*Crosses* CHARLES *to take a miniature from the wall just below fireplace. He hands it to* CHARLES.) Now, Charles, here's a chap after your own heart.
CHARLES (*steps to above the stool*). Who was he?
VICTOR. My great-great-grandfather. He ruined two men in one evening playing faro, and killed another at five o'clock the next morning. He was a fellow of the Royal Society, too.
CHARLES. He must have been quite a fellow! Why did he kill the third guy, wouldn't he pay up?
VICTOR. No, no, it was an affair of the heart.
CHARLES. A woman?
VICTOR. Oh yes, it was a woman. Gentlemen didn't fight over men in those days.
CHARLES. How did it happen?
VICTOR. He discovered his wife was about to elope with a wealthy young landowner from North Carolina. Beautiful country there, I believe. I've always wanted to see it. D'you know it at all?
CHARLES. Yes, indeed I know it well. (*Having fun.*) Still quite primitive in parts, I understand.
VICTOR (*enjoying it all*). Really. But you're not from the South yourself, are you?
CHARLES. No, I was born in New York State, but I've been around. But what happened—was he hanged?
VICTOR. No—no. It was a duel. Pistols. Somewhere near Highgate Ponds.

CHARLES. And what happened to the lady?

(VICTOR *takes miniature from* CHARLES, *hangs it back and takes down another.*)

VICTOR. My great-great-grandmother? She had several more children. Mostly by my great-great-grandfather—and they lived happily ever after.

HILARY (*acidly*). What a fascinating story. Why've you never told it me before?

VICTOR. I'm sorry, my dear, perhaps I shouldn't have mentioned it now. I've always done my best to shelter you from the unpleasant sordid side of life. She was very lovely, don't you think? (*Hands it to* CHARLES.)

CHARLES. She certainly was.

HILARY. Let me see that.

(CHARLES *hands it to her.*)

That's my great-great-grandmother.

VICTOR. No, darling, it isn't.

HILARY. Of course it is.

(VICTOR *crosses below sofa and up to sofa table, picks up his brandy and drops back to* R. *of sofa.*)

VICTOR. No it isn't. We sold yours to go to Grundelwald; you know I was only saying the other day, if the morals of this century get any worse it might be quite a good thing to reintroduce duelling. Make it legal, I mean.

HATTIE (*rises, crosses to* HILARY *above stool and takes miniature*). How would that help?

VICTOR. Cut the divorce rate in half.

HATTIE. Might cut the husbands in half, too. Then what should we do about alimony?

HILARY. You'd be a widow and get the lot.

HATTIE. Then I think it's a marvellous idea! Can't you do anything about it, Victor? (*Hangs up the second miniature.*)

VICTOR. I was just wondering. (*Up to drinks table.*) Let me give you some more brandy, Charles.

CHARLES. Thank you. (*Up to* L. *of* VICTOR.)

VICTOR (*pouring brandy*). As the government insists that nuclear weapons are a deterrent against war, then surely they'd have to accept duelling as a deterrent against divorce. Might get a Bill through the Commons on that basis. It would all depend—

HATTIE. On whether the big shots were good shots? (*She roars with laughter and sits chair chaise longue.*) Ha, ha, ha!
VICTOR (*crosses to* HATTIE *with kümmel bottle*). Hattie, more kümmel?
HATTIE. Yes, please.
VICTOR (*taking her glass*). I did warn you about Hattie, didn't I, Charles? (*Crosses back to drinks table* R. *of* CHARLES, *who drops to fireplace.*) Hilary, darling, you haven't told me what you did in London this week. Did you have fun?
HILARY. Yes, thank you.
VICTOR. What did you do?
HILARY. Oh, you know, the usual things one does in London. (HATTIE *giggles*.) Oh! That reminds me—
VICTOR. Of what? (*Crosses down* R. *of sofa with his brandy.*)
HILARY. Well I—I say, I do hope you're not going to be stuffy and say I've been dishonest.
VICTOR (*sits in armchair*). Stuffy! You make me sound like a bed-sitting room. What have you done?
HILARY. Well, one morning—
VICTOR. A long time ago in the beautiful old city of Hamelin—that's your voice for children's stories, Hilary. I don't trust it.
HILARY (*annoyed, goes back to normal*). I found a cloakroom ticket for a taxi in a suitcase.
VICTOR. That can't be right.
HILARY. I mean I found a cloakroom ticket for a suitcase in a taxi.
VICTOR. You did?
HILARY. Yes.
VICTOR. So of course you gave it to the driver.
HILARY. No, I didn't, I'm afraid.
VICTOR. Now, Hilary, you're not going to tell me you went and got it out?
HILARY. Yes, I did.
VICTOR. How thoroughly disgraceful! Where was it?
   (VICTOR *rises to back of sofa,* CHARLES *and* HATTIE *are studying the miniatures and mantelpiece most intently.*)
HILARY. Victoria, Victor. Which seemed a sort of omen. There was an awful lot to pay on it. It had been there for simply ages. So I thought the person might have died or something.
HATTIE. Or it might have been stolen property and the thief got windy and dumped it there. My God! There wasn't a body in it, was there? (*Sits on stool facing* VICTOR.)

HILARY. I don't know.
VICTOR. What d'you mean you don't know?
HILARY. It's locked and none of my keys would fit. I haven't opened it yet.
VICTOR. Charles, d'you hear this astounding confession?
CHARLES (*he is looking at the mantelpiece*). I'm trying not to.
VICTOR. That's very good of you. I appreciate it. I must say I'm astonished at you, Hilary. I mean short changing the public when they pay their entrance money, and selling old mushrooms as fresh—that's one thing, but you've never done anything criminal before.
HILARY. It's not criminal. I found the ticket. I didn't steal it.
VICTOR. The fact remains, you're in possession of someone else's property. Well now, what are we going to do? Obviously we ought to return it, but we can't do that without getting involved with the police—officials, and the National Press. All of whom I'm very frightened of.
HATTIE. What's the point of returning it now? You'd never get it back to the proper owner. Anyway he shouldn't have been so careless as to lose the ticket.
VICTOR (*puts brandy on sofa table*). And it would end up as lost property. (*Back to behind sofa.*) I suppose the first thing to do is to find out what's inside it. Let's hope it's nothing of value. (HILARY *and* HATTIE *catch each other's eye.*) Where is it?
HILARY. It's in my room.
VICTOR. I'll get my keys and see if they're any good. And I'll tell Sellars to bring it down. (*Crosses above armchair to* D.R. *door, then turns.*) Charles—Hattie.
HATTIE. What, darling?
VICTOR (*back to behind sofa*). Not the least embarrassing part of Hilary's behaviour is that I must ask you to promise me—not only for her sake but for mine as well—not to repeat what's happened and to try to forget all about it.
HATTIE. Of course we promise. Don't we?
CHARLES. Why, yes, sure. It's forgotten.
VICTOR. We're very grateful, aren't we, darling?
HILARY. I'm very sorry. I should never have done it, I know, but—
VICTOR. Of course you shouldn't have done it, but d'you know something? I have a horrible feeling I should have done the same thing myself. (*Crosses back to* D.R. *door.*)

HATTIE. I must say I think it's all rather exciting.
VICTOR. Really, Hattie, you talk as if Hilary had won some money from Littlewoods. (*Exit.*)
HATTIE. It's the mink of course.
HILARY. Yes.
HATTIE. My dear, what a perfectly brilliant idea. He fell for it hook, line and sinker.
HILARY (*almost in tears*). Oh, Hattie, I feel so awful. And I'm so hopeless at lying.
HATTIE. You're not doing so badly.
HILARY. And he was so sweet about it, wasn't he?
CHARLES (*drops to D.S. of stool*). Listen, Hattie, go and powder your nose—will you?—I've got to talk to Hilary. And if you can find Victor, keep him away as long as possible.
HATTIE (*rising and kissing* HILARY). Now you mustn't be upset, my sweet. (*Looking from one to the other.*) Oh dear, I feel (*Crossing below armchair.*) just like Friar Lawrence. (*Exit, leaving door open.*)
CHARLES (*round above sofa, shuts D.R. door*). Come here.
HILARY (*rises, back to the fire*). No. And you stay where you are.
CHARLES. Why?
HILARY. I can't think clearly when I'm near you.
CHARLES (*at R.C.*). What d'you mean?
HILARY. You know exactly what I mean. D'you remember saying that to me? You were standing just there.
CHARLES. Darling, I've had enough. I can't take this any longer. Don't tell me, I know . . . it's my own fault. I insisted on coming, I know that. It meant two days with you. Now I know that he knows. He knows that I know he knows. He knows that you know he knows. And Hattie knows. We all know we all know. A top secret we all know. Like the day before D-Day. Well the hell with the top secret.
HILARY. What d'you mean?
CHARLES. Let's come clean. Let me talk to him.
HILARY. No, you made a promise.
CHARLES. And I think I've decided to break it.
HILARY. Darling, no, please, please no. You must think of me.
CHARLES. I haven't thought of anything else since the moment I set eyes on you. (*Begins to move slowly towards her.*)
HILARY. Stay where you are.
CHARLES (*retreating, infuriated*). Now listen, Victor knows all about it.

Does he seem upset? Does he seem jealous? Does he appear to care one way or another? (*He waits.*) Answer me.

HILARY. Of course he cares. But he's not a very jealous person.

CHARLES. Well, in his position he ought to be jealous. I don't think he gives a damn.

HILARY. Yes, he ought to be a little bit jealous, oughtn't he? Hattie asked him if he'd considered the possibility of my running away with you and d'you know what he said?

CHARLES. What?

HILARY. He said he thought it would be a pity. A pity!

CHARLES. Well, there you are. If he really cared, if you were really important to him, d'you imagine for one moment he'd have asked me down here? Of course he wouldn't. Not unless he's a lunatic.

HILARY. No, he's not a lunatic. But he's never really been quite like other boys. This may be his way of saying—"All right, I understand. We don't have to talk about it or discuss it. Just as long as you stay here, that's all".

CHARLES. D'you honestly believe that?

HILARY. I'm in such a muddle, darling, I don't know what I believe.

CHARLES. Well, I know what I believe. I believe you love me. I believe I could make you happy. And I believe without upsetting Victor a very great deal, you could get a divorce and marry me.

HILARY. Perhaps you don't understand Englishmen very well.

CHARLES. Who does?

HILARY. English women.

CHARLES. Darling, we're wasting precious time.

HILARY. Then kiss me.

CHARLES. How can I? You're too far away.

HILARY. Then come here.

CHARLES. You told me not to.

HILARY. I've changed my mind.

CHARLES. Does that mean you'll marry me?

HILARY. No. Oh, Charles, darling, can't you see—?

CHARLES. I shall talk to him as soon as you've gone to bed.

HILARY (*kneels on sofa, leaning over the back*). He may guess what you're going to say and head you off by going to bed himself.

CHARLES. I can make it so he can't. And if things go the way I think they will, I'll stay here and we can all discuss it in the morning. If he acts up I'll drive back to London tonight. I'll cancel my plans and arrange to stay in England all summer.

HILARY. You're so beautifully determined; no wonder I'm in love with you.
CHARLES (*steps to her and leans on back of sofa*). If I'm not here tomorrow, will you call me?
HILARY. No.
CHARLES. We've had this conversation before.
HILARY. We keep doing that, don't we?
CHARLES. Remember?
HILARY. Only a week ago.
CHARLES. For me it was a week with only four days in it. Oh, Hilary, darling! I could give you such a lovely life.
HILARY. I was having quite a lovely life before you came into it.
CHARLES. Will you call me?
HILARY. I suppose I will—just like I did the first time I said I wouldn't.
CHARLES. Does that mean you'll change your mind?
HILARY. I don't know what I shall do with my mind. I'm not really in a fit state to be in charge of it. Someone else ought to drive it for me, park it somewhere and then later on, when you've gone away, I'll go and collect it.

(HATTIE *enters to below armchair.* HILARY *rises to sit on chair chaise longue.* CHARLES *crosses below sofa to fireplace.*)

HATTIE. It's coming down, with Sellars.
VICTOR (*entering to* R. *of sofa*). Now, one of these ought to fit it.

(HATTIE *does a loud yawn and curls up in the chair.*)

Oh yes, darling, Hattie says she's tired. I expect you are, too, after your week in London.
HILARY (*looking at* CHARLES). It was four days, not a week.
VICTOR. Charles, I thought if they're going to leave us and go to bed, you and I might have a game of billiards; it's quite early yet. Would you like to?
CHARLES. Yes, I would. But I warn you I don't know your English game.
VICTOR. I'm not sure I do very clearly, but we can make it up as we go along. (*Sits on back of sofa.*)
HILARY. Perhaps Charles doesn't want to play. Why don't we all have an early night?
CHARLES. No, I'd like to play.
VICTOR. Good! And we'll take the brandy with us.
HATTIE. That means they'll finish up playing Billiard Fives.

(SELLARS *enters above armchair to* R.C., *puts case down.* HATTIE *and* HILARY *rise.*)

VICTOR. Ah, there you are, Sellars. Bring it over here. That's it, now try some of these. (*Hands the keys to* SELLARS, *who sets to work.*)

HATTIE (*trying to lift it*). It's heavy, isn't it?

HILARY. Heavy?

HATTIE (*looking at the labels*). You couldn't really get a body in there, could you? Not unless it was cut up, of course.

VICTOR. Don't be disgusting.

HATTIE. All right then—dismembered.

VICTOR. That sounds worse.

HATTIE. I expect that's why the papers always use it.

VICTOR. Put it up here, Sellars, you'll find it easier. (SELLARS *puts it on the* D.S. *arm of the sofa, crossing below* VICTOR.) That's better, isn't it?

SELLARS. Yes, milord.

HATTIE (R. *of* VICTOR). It's a shabby old case—can't have belonged to anyone very posh!

VICTOR. Posh! Dismembered! Really, Hattie, your vocabulary's most bizarre.

HATTIE (*crossing below* VICTOR *to* R. *of* SELLARS). But then, so am I, darling. I was just thinking, perhaps it's not to be opened till Christmas.

SELLARS. Or maybe it's like Pandora's Box, madam, and we shouldn't open it at all! Ah! There it is.

(*The lid of the suitcase flies open and out fall a cricket bat, three old cricket pads, some London telephone directories etc. Only a string of flags lies in the bottom.*)

HILARY. Oh!

HATTIE. I told you it didn't belong to anyone very posh.

HILARY *and* HATTIE *each take an end of the flags from the case and start pulling out the rows of flags as*

THE CURTAIN FALLS.

Scene 2

Later the same night.

As the curtain rises the stage is empty. The lights on mantelpiece are on and the fire is still burning. The U.L. *door is open.* VICTOR'S *dinner jacket is over back of sofa with his spectacles in the breast pocket.*

CHARLES' *dinner jacket is over back of desk chair with spectacles in pocket.*

SELLARS' *coat is on desk.* CHARLES *enters from the door leading to the public rooms. He is without his coat and is carrying a Lüger pistol. He goes to the drinks table, then glances round the room looking for the brandy.*

SELLARS, *in his shirtsleeves, enters by same door to* L. *of sofa table.*

SELLARS. His lordship's waiting, sir. Are you looking for anything, sir?
CHARLES. I was looking for the brandy, Sellars.
SELLARS. His lordship's got it up the other end of the corridor, sir.
CHARLES. Oh!
SELLARS. I'll fetch it, sir, if you feel in need of it.
CHARLES. Thank you, Sellars. (*Reluctantly going to exit* U.L.) No, no, don't bother. Maybe I'll do better without it.
SELLARS (*back to* L. *of sofa table*). You were lucky to win the toss, sir. That Lüger's a far better job than the three-eight his lordship's got.
VICTOR (*off*). Come on! What are you doing?
    (CHARLES *puts pistol on the desk.*)
SELLARS (*calling round the door* U.L.). Just going over the procedure again, milord, with Mr. Delacro.
    (CHARLES *takes off his tie.*)
VICTOR (*off*). Well, buck up! It's draughty here.
SELLARS (*back to* L. *of sofa table*). Now, are you quite clear about the drill, sir? I shall count one, two, three, and on the word fire you turn and shoot.
CHARLES. O.K. Thank you, Sellars.
VICTOR (*off*). Sellars, I think I'd better have my spectacles.
    (CHARLES *puts his tie over desk chair, takes his spectacles from coat pocket, cleans them with handkerchief.*)

SELLARS (*crossing back to* U.L. *door*). Very good, milord. (*Looking on mantelpiece.*) Where are they?
VICTOR (*off*). They're in my coat.
   (SELLARS *kneels on sofa and takes spectacles from coat which is over back of sofa. He then crosses to* U.L. *door and turns back to* CHARLES.)
SELLARS. Good luck, sir.
CHARLES. Thank you, Sellars.
SELLARS. As I'm also his lordship's second, I shall of course wish him good luck, too, sir. (*Exit.*)
CHARLES. But of course.
   (CHARLES *puts on his spectacles, picks up the Lüger, clicks his heels and goes out* L.)
SELLARS (*off*). Now, gentlemen, are you both absolutely clear as to procedure? (*Pause.*) I shall repeat it once more. I shall count one, two, three, and on the command fire you turn and shoot. Any questions? Good. Now one further detail. Are there any messages, milord?
VICTOR (*off*). I should like you to have my cuff links, Sellars.
SELLARS (*off*). Thank you, milord.
CHARLES (*off*). You can have my Cadillac, Sellars. The keys are on my dressing table.
SELLARS (*off*). That's very good of you. Thank you, sir. Now, gentlemen! On your marks, please. Check your safety catches. Get ready. One—two—three. Fire!
   (*Two deafening shots are exchanged, followed instantly by a tremendous crash, as of some heavy object falling and smashing.*)
(*Off.*) Oh dear, oh dear, oh dear!
   (*There is absolute silence.*)
VICTOR (*off*). Well, it doesn't look as though you'll get my cuff links, Sellars.
SELLARS (*off*). No, milord. Are you all right, Mr. Delacro?
VICTOR (*off*). Come on, let's get back to the fire. Sellars, don't forget the brandy.
   (VICTOR *enters to above the chaise longue stool. He has a small hole in his shirt and a certain amount of blood shows at the top of his* L. *arm. He still has the three-eight revolver.*)
      (CHARLES *enters with the Lüger, drops to below* VICTOR L. *of him, looking at the wound.* SELLARS *enters, takes a look at* VICTOR'S *arm, goes out again, turns out the lights in the passage and re-enters with brandy.*)
CHARLES. Are you all right? Let me look at that.

VICTOR. Yes, quite all right. It's only a scratch. Will you enter me up in your game book, Charles? Under various, I suppose.

(VICTOR *drops* L. *of stool to below it.* SELLARS *switches on lights below* U.L. *door. The three table lamps come on.*)

CHARLES (*examining gun*). I can't understand this, it must fire way off to the left.

(SELLARS *crosses above sofa table with brandy to desk and lifts telephone receiver.*)

VICTOR. What are you doing, Sellars?

SELLARS. Telephoning the doctor, milord.

VICTOR. Well, don't. Put that thing down.

(*Sits* D.S. *side of stool* SELLARS *puts down telephone and brandy, puts on his coat.* CHARLES *puts pistol on back of sofa.*)

CHARLES. Now don't be absurd, you've got to have a doctor.

VICTOR. Of course I've got to have a doctor—I know that. Sellars, give me a very large brandy. I do beg your pardon, Charles, give us both a very large brandy.

SELLARS. Would you mind if I had one too, milord? I'm feeling a little faint. (*Picks up brandy, comes behind sofa doing up his coat.*)

VICTOR. My God! I didn't hit you, did I, Sellars?

SELLARS. No, milord. You hit a marble bust of George the Fourth at the end of the corridor. (*Behind sofa with brandy.*)

(VICTOR *sits on chair of chaise longue and puts feet on stool.* SELLARS *to drinks table, pours two brandies.*)

VICTOR. Oh, what a great pity. I was rather attached to it. But it was quite an understandable mistake, your features are very alike. And now you'll be able to tell your friends you once had your life saved by a king of England. Better not mention which one or they'll think you're the Flying Dutchman.

CHARLES. Now look here, I'm afraid I'm going to insist on calling that doctor. You can't just sit around here with a bullet hole in you, drinking brandy. You may not feel much at the moment, but that's going to hurt later on. (*Crosses between* U.S. *end of sofa and sofa table to telephone.*)

VICTOR. Yes, I daresay, but to get him on the telephone would be a mistake, and I'd rather you didn't.

CHARLES. What's his number?

VICTOR. I shan't tell you. They exchange a twenty-four hour monitoring system. (SELLARS *hands* VICTOR *his brandy, then* CHARLES *his.*)

Thank you. (*Raising his glass to* CHARLES.) Foolish as it may sound, I drink to your continued good health.

CHARLES. I drink to shooting and fishing.

VICTOR. And to George the Fourth, surely. Sellars, you'll have to clean these guns. I'm afraid I can't manage them.

(SELLARS *picks up revolver from stool, then kneels on sofa and picks up the pistol from back of it.*

HATTIE *enters* D.R., *sees* SELLARS *with pistols, screams, holds up her hands and hides behind the armchair. She is followed immediately by* HILARY.)

HILARY (*below armchair*). What's happening?

HATTIE. They're all wearing glasses.

(VICTOR *and* CHARLES *take off their glasses.*)

HILARY. Sellars, what's the matter with you?

SELLARS. Nothing at all, milady.

HILARY (*slowly up to back of sofa*). Now, Sellars, nobody's going to hurt you. You're not to be frightened, we're all friends here. Victor, can't you do something?

(VICTOR *and* CHARLES *laugh.*)

VICTOR. You've got the wrong end of the stick, darling. He's only going to clean them, isn't he, Charles?

(CHARLES *starts to put on his tie.*)

HILARY. Victor, what's the matter with your arm? (*Below sofa sits on stool chaise longue looking at the blood on* VICTOR'S *shirt.*) What have you done? What's been happening?

VICTOR. Charles and I had a duel. I missed him.

HILARY. A duel. Don't be ridiculous.

VICTOR. I'm not being ridiculous, it's perfectly true.

HATTIE (*drops to* D.C.). We thought you'd started *Son et Lumière.*

HILARY. You and Charles fought a duel?

VICTOR. Yes.

HILARY. You must be out of your mind. Supposing you'd woken Emma.

VICTOR. Don't be so unromantic.

HILARY. Duelling. (*Crosses below sofa.*) I've never heard of anything so absolutely preposterous. You're the Earl of Rhyall, not the Count of Monte Cristo. Hattie, call the doctor, will you, his number's two nine. (HATTIE *up to telephone.*) I do apologize, Sellars. (*Exit* D.R., *crossing below armchair.*)

SELLARS. A very natural mistake, milady.

(SELLARS *rises and puts guns on sofa table, the revolver at the* R. *end, then goes to drinks table and helps himself to a brandy.*)
VICTOR. No, Hattie, don't. If we call him on the telephone the exchange will listen in to the conversation, and by tomorrow morning the whole damn village will know, and by the evening it will be in the papers. Somebody better fetch him.
CHARLES (*crossing below* HATTIE *to* D.R. *door, putting on his coat*). I'll go.
VICTOR. Thank you, that would be very kind.
HATTIE. Well, that's the least he can do. (*Comes to back of sofa.*) Anyway, you're not supposed to have a duel without a doctor. In the pictures he's always the one with a bag, and without a beard.
CHARLES (*to above armchair*). Where does he live?
VICTOR. In the village, same side as the church. He's got a magnolia tree in the garden, and his brass plate on the gate—you can't miss it.
(CHARLES *starts to go.*)
CHARLES (*back above armchair*). How do I get to the village?
HATTIE. I know the way—I'll come with you. Wait two minutes while I put something on. (*Crossing to* VICTOR.) You look frightfully romantic, but you are all right, darling?
VICTOR. Perfectly all right, thank you.
HATTIE. Honest?
VICTOR. Honest.
HATTIE. Had we better tell the doctor to send for an ambulance?
VICTOR. Certainly not, I'm staying here. Tell him there's been a slight accident. (SELLARS *pulls sofa round to its Act One position.*) You'll have to explain what it is, but say I'm pretty sure it's nothing serious and only a flesh wound.
HATTIE. How shall we say it happened?
SELLARS. Excuse me, milord, would you be more comfortable here?
(VICTOR *rises and sits* L. *end of sofa.* SELLARS *is at* R. *end.* HATTIE *at* L. *end.*)
VICTOR. Tell him my butler, who is a highly nervous man, mistook me for a burglar and took a shot at me. You don't mind, do you, Sellars?
SELLARS. Not at all, milord. (*Up to above sofa table with* VICTOR'S *coat, then crosses to fire, puts a log on it.*)
CHARLES. Is he going to believe it?
VICTOR. He's a nice chap, but a snob, they always believe anything. The police have their Fête in the grounds here in July, so they'll have to believe it, too.

HATTIE (*kissing* VICTOR's *cheek*). You are clever. You think of everything, don't you?

CHARLES. Come on, Hattie, we ought to get going.

HATTIE. You wait here, Charles. I'll give you a shout when I'm ready.

(*Crosses below sofa to on stage of armchair just as* HILARY *enters with* VICTOR's *dressing-gown, bowl, cotton wool, bandages and scissors.*)

Victor wouldn't let me telephone the doctor, so Charles and I are going to fetch him.

(CHARLES *sits on arm of armchair.*)

HILARY. Be as quick as you can, won't you? (*Crossing below sofa to* L. *end, she puts bowl with cotton wool, bandage and scissors in it and dressing-gown on end of sofa.*)

HATTIE. Yes, darling, of course. (*Exit.*)

HILARY (*begins attending to his wound*). I heard a terrific crash as well as the shots—was that you falling?

VICTOR. No, that was George the Fourth, whom I mistook for Charles.

HILARY (*cutting open the seam joining the sleeve to the shirt*). Then you're not damaged anywhere else?

VICTOR. No, darling.

HILARY. Am I hurting?

(SELLARS *at fire, having put a log on.*)

VICTOR. No, darling. You needn't wait any longer, Sellars, and thank you for all your help.

SELLARS (*crosses below sofa and armchair with* VICTOR's *coat*). No, no, no, milord.

VICTOR (*to* HILARY). Sellars acted as second to both of us, and conducted the whole thing quite admirably.

HILARY. Sellars, would you get a hot-water bottle, please?

SELLARS. Yes, milady. (*Exit* D.R.)

CHARLES (*rises*). I don't think it's bad, is it?

HILARY. I don't think it is, luckily, but I can't really tell.

CHARLES (*leaning over* R. *arm of sofa*). How are you feeling?

VICTOR. Like another brandy.

HILARY (*firmly*). No.

VICTOR. Hilary, I warn you if you talk like that I shall finish the bottle. (*Hands his glass to* CHARLES.) Thank you, Charles.

CHARLES (*gets brandy from drinks table, brings it to sofa table and pours it out*). I suppose I am just as much to blame as he is, but I really had no alternative. I tried to talk to him, but he merely kept repeating his challenge. If I accepted he promised to discuss the whole thing afterwards.

HILARY. Supposing one of you'd been killed, or both of you.

VICTOR. Precisely. Pointless to discuss it before.

CHARLES. On the other hand, if I refused I was to return to London immediately. (*Puts brandy on drinks table.*)

(HILARY *has finished her bandage and helps* VICTOR *into his dressing gown.*)

VICTOR (*rises*). Thank you. Well, go on, tell her the rest.

CHARLES. He called Sellars in, repeated the challenge in front of him and said if I didn't accept in five minutes, he'd tell him to telephone the press, and give them an eye-witness account of the whole story.

VICTOR. What the butler saw in stereoscopic sound. He really had no choice, did he, darling? (*Taking brandy from* CHARLES.) Thank you so much. (HILARY *is doing up his dressing-gown; his* L. *arm is not through the sleeve.*)

HILARY. Why didn't you miss him? He missed you.

CHARLES. Well, goddamit, I nearly missed him.

VICTOR. That wouldn't have done any good, anyway. According to the Sellars' rules, you start at thirty paces. (*Sits* L. *end of sofa.*) If you both miss you advance five yards and fire again. You get three shots in all. Rather like darts, only you move nearer each time.

HATTIE (*calling off*). Hurry up, Charles, I'm waiting.

CHARLES. I'll be right back. (*Crossing above armchair. Exit.*)

VICTOR. The West Corridor was long enough, of course, but one felt rather cramped. We wanted to have it outside, but that would have meant waiting until it was light, and I didn't want to keep Sellars up. Besides, we might have been rather drunk by then.

HILARY. I think you're drunk now. (*Crossing above sofa with bowl, scissors, cotton wool. Puts them on desk.*)

VICTOR. I never drink when I'm duelling.

(*Enter* D.R. SELLARS *with bottle, glasses and a white cloth. Crosses above arm-chair to above sofa table.*)

HILARY. What on earth have you got there, Sellars?

SELLARS (*putting glasses on sofa table*). The champagne his lordship ordered.

VICTOR. Oh, thank you. Open it, will you, Sellars?

HILARY (*on stage of desk chair*). When did you order champagne?

VICTOR. When did I order it, Sellars?

SELLARS. Earlier this evening, milord.
HILARY. Why?
VICTOR. I thought we might need it.
HILARY. Have we anything to celebrate?
VICTOR. I thought we might get thirsty, I got it from the grocers'. (*The cork comes out.*) I hope it's all right.
HILARY. On my bill, I suppose.
VICTOR. I'll pay you back.
HILARY (*understanding his real reason*). You really got it to be friendly, didn't you?
VICTOR. You have a wonderful gift of choosing the right word.
      (SELLARS *comes to* R. *end of sofa, hands them each a glass and leaves bottle on sofa table.*)
HILARY (*taking glass*). Thank you, Sellars.
VICTOR (*taking his glass*). Thank you, have a glass yourself.
SELLARS (*crossing below* HILARY *to* D.R. *door*). No thank you, milord. (*At door.*) As I've served his lordship's cold bottle, milady, I'll now go and attend to his hot one. (*Exit.*)
VICTOR. Good luck. (*He drinks but she does not.*) Come on, drink up. I'm glad you thought it friendly.
HILARY (*crossing to on stage of desk chair*). I'm sorry about this, Victor. Very, very sorry.
VICTOR. Then drown your sorrow.
HILARY. I'm not sure I can.
VICTOR. You're not cross with me, are you?
HILARY. No, I'm not cross—I just think you should see a doctor.
VICTOR. But I am going to see a doctor.
HILARY. Not him. I mean a specialist. A brain specialist for mental disorders. D'you realize you might have been killed, or disabled for life, or put in prison for manslaughter?
VICTOR. You should be flattered I risked so much for you.
HILARY. Well, I'm not. I'm shocked and disgusted.
VICTOR. How very ungracious of you.
HILARY (*crossing above sofa to fire*). I thought you were an intelligent, civilized person and you behave like a barbarian.
VICTOR. Oh come now, you can't call the elder Pitt a barbarian, or Sheridan, or Canning, or Byron or even the Iron Duke. They were all duellists. Besides, what else do you expect me to do with an American millionaire who, with half a crown's worth of aid to Britain, walks into my house and disrupts my life?

HILARY. I'm just as much to blame as he is. (*Sits up stage edge of stool facing audience.*) Listen, Victor, I know I've behaved disgracefully, but let me try and explain what's happened to me.
VICTOR. We know that. You've fallen in love.
HILARY. For the past week I've been more or less sort of schizophrenic, and feeling so sorry for that poor little squirrel.
VICTOR. What on earth are you talking about?
HILARY. Your squirrel with two heads. Don't you remember? Poor chap, I know how miserable he must have felt. I've got two heads myself now.
VICTOR. They're both very pretty heads.
HILARY. One is appalled by my behaviour, the other approves it. Two of my eyes are dazzled, bewitched and so happy, the other two have tears in them. I can't explain it any other way, and I don't expect you to understand it.
VICTOR. But of course I understand it. And I'm only so grateful to you for not saying "This is something stronger than I am".
HILARY. Well, if you want the plain, honest truth, that's exactly what it was.
VICTOR. Why the past tense?
HILARY. Because it is in the past tense. (*Rises round* L. *end of sofa to above it.*) Not that you appear to give a damn about it anyway.
VICTOR. What makes you say that?
HILARY. From what I gather from Hattie, all you said was you thought it was a pity. (*Pours them each some more champagne and comes to* R. *end of sofa.*)
VICTOR. Ah no, I said I thought it'd be a pity if you ran away with Charles. I can't see you in what's called the international set, my darling. (HILARY *wanders to* R.C.) Not the glitter and glare of St. Moritz and Palm Beach and Nassau. You're English and you need the gentleness of the rain and the soft winds of England.
HILARY. And a nest of robins in my hair.
VICTOR. Besides you'd be wearing sun glasses all the year round and nobody would see the colour of your eyes. That'd be a very great pity.
HILARY. Anyway, who's suggesting such a life for me?
VICTOR. Charles is, isn't he? I suppose you'd have someone to pack for you.
HILARY. And that's the only reason you think it would be a pity?
VICTOR. No, no, certainly not. I can think of a thousand pities.

HILARY. But none from your point of view?
VICTOR. Oh yes, indeed. But let's not go into that.
HILARY. Why not?
VICTOR. Because this is hardly the moment. Let's just say I should miss going to bed with you, and there'd be nobody to do the Christmas cards.

(HILARY *crosses up* R. *of sofa, sits on stool below window which has been set one foot* D.S. *of original position for this scene*.)

HILARY. You seem to overlook the fact that if you hadn't invited Charles here for the week-end I should already have said good-bye to him, and the whole thing might have been finished and done with.
VICTOR. Unfinished and done with. Very different. A most unsatisfactory state of affairs for all concerned.
HILARY. And you think you've saved us all from that by getting yourself shot up in a duel.
VICTOR. Not at all. Though I admit the duel was an essential part of an effort to try and preserve our marriage.
HILARY. I'm a little confused. From the way you've been talking, I imagined you were hell bent and hot foot for the Divorce Court.
VICTOR. Who said anything about divorce? I never mentioned it. I don't like divorce. I like marriage. I mean, it's like the boat race, you've got to pick one or the other, haven't you? And I'll tell you something else—I don't think adultery sufficient grounds for it.
HILARY (*rises and goes round behind sofa to fireplace*). What a masculine attitude!
VICTOR. I don't think marriage is just a liaison to be terminated when the sexual side of it becomes boring or irksome to either party. (*Moves to* R. *end of sofa and puts his feet up, moving champagne bottle from sofa table to floor beside him*.)
HILARY. It's never been boring or irksome. Not for me it hasn't. (*Kneels* U.S. *of stool leaning on it facing audience*.) And don't talk about "either party". It makes the whole thing sound like a contract.
VICTOR. When two people make promises, what else can it be but a contract? You promised to be faithful. Well, you've broken that one. Am I to respond by breaking one of mine? To have and to hold from this day forth for better for worse. This moment in our lives must obviously come under the heading "for worse". And the popular measure taken nowadays is to say "Well, the better part of it's over and here we are with the worse, so good-bye, my dear,

thank you so much. It was fun while it lasted. You take your boy friend, I'll take my freedom, and I'll be on the Riviera before you". Well, I think that's wrong. If your mistress is unfaithful, she should be discarded. If your wife is, she should be befriended.

HILARY. Befriended? Meaning helped and patronized?

VICTOR. Meaning beloved and cherished. Unless she's a promiscuous trollop, of course, then the situation is out of control and quite hopeless.

HILARY. I'm not a promiscuous trollop, and it's never happened before.

VICTOR. I didn't say you were and I know it hasn't.

HILARY. It has with you.

VICTOR (*loudly*). Objection!

HILARY. Objection overruled. How do I know you're not a promiscuous—whatever the masculine is of trollop?

VICTOR (*picks up bottle and pours her some more, then himself*). The same way you know I don't like French mustard or going to the opera—because we've been living together for twelve years.

HILARY. I wonder why "living together" sounds so much more fun than if you'd said married for twelve years?

VICTOR. To me it doesn't. I think marriage is great fun—thank you very much. (*Pause, then very sincerely.*) That thank you very much, by the way, wasn't just a figure of speech, it meant I'm very grateful to you for having made it fun. I thought perhaps now was the right moment to say thank you.

HILARY (*a little affected*). Ditto, ditto—as we used to say.

VICTOR. Now I find myself up a bit of a gum tree.

HILARY. Why?

(*Enter* SELLARS D.R. *with hot-water bottle.*)

SELLARS. The hot-water bottle, milady.

HILARY. Thank you. (*Takes it from* SELLARS *just below* R. *end of sofa and puts it behind* VICTOR'S *back.*)

SELLARS. I'm sorry we didn't have a—how shall I put it?—a home win, milord.

VICTOR. I'm sorry we kept you up so late, Sellars, and thank you.

SELLARS. That's all right, milord, and it's I should be thanking you really. I've learnt a great deal from events this evening. (*Crosses to* D.R. *door.*)

HILARY. What have you learnt, Sellars?

SELLARS. Amongst other things, that my novel's no good, milady.

HILARY. Oh—?

SELLARS. I'm about to go upstairs and tear it up. (*Opens the door.*) It's not true to life at all. (*Exit.*)

VICTOR. How can any one say what's true to life? Now where was I?

HILARY (*sits on the floor between sofa and stool*). Up a gum tree.

VICTOR. Oh yes. And very uncomfortable, too, because the role of complaisant husband I find distasteful and the jealous one rather ludicrous. In point of fact—much to my annoyance—I turn out to be both.

HILARY. Are you jealous?

VICTOR. Very.

HILARY. It would be rather hurtful if you weren't.

VICTOR. Then you must feel very gratified.

HILARY. Yes, I do, thank you, darling. Are you quite sure you're jealous?

VICTOR. Yes, I am quite sure. Why?

HILARY. I wondered if it wasn't just a sense of possession that had been aroused in you. Like losing something that belonged to you.

VICTOR. Like the contents of a suitcase? No, it's a little more than that.

HILARY (*tapping his leg*). Where is it?

VICTOR. Where is what?

HILARY. You know damn well what. Come on, where is it?

VICTOR. I really haven't the faintest idea what on earth you're talking about.

HILARY. We're talking about the contents of a suitcase.

VICTOR. Oh. Oh, but that was merely, as I said before, a figure of speech. Hadn't you better go and put a little make-up on?

HILARY (*infuriated*). Why the hell should I put make-up on—for Doctor Fenton?

VICTOR. No, of course not. For Charles. I'm used to seeing you like that; he probably isn't. You don't want to distress him. (HILARY, *furious, takes a drink.*) Not that you're not looking most attractive. I always rather like you like that, but he may have different ideas, my darling. (HILARY *crawls across his legs and takes the champagne bottle, pours herself some more.*) I suppose really I shouldn't call you my darling. That again has become merely a figure of speech. I think I'd better have some more champagne, this is beginning to hurt.

HILARY. Are you all right?

VICTOR. Yes, thank you.

HILARY (*pouring it into his glass*). Now drink that up and let me get you into bed.

(*Rises round* L. *end of sofa and puts bottle on sofa table, then stays at* L. *end of sofa.*)

VICTOR. Despite the fact I'm your husband, in the present circumstances I find that a most improper suggestion. (*Throws hot-water bottle on to chair chaise longue.*)

HILARY. You may have talked a certain amount of sense, but there's been an awful lot of hot air, too, you know.

VICTOR. Nonsense. It's all been sense. What d'you mean—hot air?

HILARY. About my needing the softness of the winds and the gentleness of the rain. (*Picks up hot-water bottle.*) Do you remember last winter when we couldn't get out of here because the softness of the English winds had blown three lime trees down across the drive, and the gentleness of the rain had flooded the cellars and all my mushrooms? Incidentally, do you think I like growing mushrooms? D'you think I really like living in a few rooms of an enormous damp mansion? And you know you're wrong about the international set. I think I should simply adore them; I've always longed to meet them. I could water-ski and aqua-lung, instead of that well-known English pastime of making both ends meet. (*Sits in armchair.*) It'd be so wonderful for the children, too, wouldn't it? (*There is no response from* VICTOR.) Surely you must see it's very tempting?

VICTOR. Oh, yes indeed. The grass is always greener the other side of the hedge, isn't it? No, you ought to think it over very carefully.

HILARY. Oh, I have. (VICTOR *looks at her rather quickly.*) Perhaps I still am.

VICTOR. Well, if that's what you want I shall have to think again.

HILARY. But what I can't understand is why you had to fight a duel?

VICTOR. To make my role of complaisant husband a little less—ignoble, I think the word is—and my proposition a little less disgraceful.

HILARY. What proposition?

VICTOR. Also to—to remind you I'm very fond of you. I didn't want to write you a letter or send you roses. I thought a duel was just the ticket.

HILARY (*angrily*). Just the ticket! Where to? A crematorium?

VICTOR. No, no. A cloakroom.

HILARY. Shut up! (*Rises to* R. *end of sofa.*) And what would have happened if you'd killed Charles? What d'you think I'd have done? (*Puts glass on sofa table and crosses above sofa table. Puts hot-water bottle back on chair chaise longue.*)

VICTOR. Well, now I'll let you into a secret. I'm a very reliable shot—even with a revolver.
HILARY. Well, go on.
VICTOR. Go on what?
HILARY. What's your proposition?
VICTOR. Well, I suggest that we declare a sort of moratorium.
HILARY. How d'you mean?
VICTOR. An armistice—an intermission—lunch break, call it what you like. (HILARY *sits* L. *end sofa*.) You go off with your damn millionaire. I'll wait here till you come back.
HILARY. For how long?
VICTOR. Two or three months.
HILARY. Ah! yes, I see. And—and wash that man right out of my hair? Is that the idea?
VICTOR. I think the next line was "and send him on his way". (*Rises and crosses below* HILARY *to put glass on mantelpiece*.) Which I sincerely hope you'll do—bloody tourist! Let him go sight-seeing somewhere else.
HILARY. You really mean you'd be prepared to loan me to another man for three months in order to get him out of my system?
VICTOR. Yes, shocking as it may seem, I think it's the safest route.
HILARY. To back where we were?
VICTOR. To back where we were.
HILARY. You must love me very much.
VICTOR. Love and like and value.
HILARY. Supposing it doesn't work out like that?
VICTOR. That's a chance I have to take, because it's the only one I've got.
HILARY. Yes, it is, isn't it. I can see why you call it a disgraceful proposition, but it has its points. (*Her thoughts suddenly interrupted*.) Promise you'll take me back.
VICTOR. I promise.
HILARY. And if at the end of two or three months I want a divorce to marry Charles, you'd be agreeable?
VICTOR. On the contrary, I'd be very disagreeable.
HILARY. That doesn't answer my question.
     (VICTOR *crosses below* HILARY *to* R. *end of sofa and faces her, back to the audience*.)
VICTOR. Let's discuss it when the time comes.
HILARY. And you don't want to take me back now?

VICTOR (*looks at her for a moment or two, then shakes his head*). No.
HILARY. Why not?
VICTOR. You're too attractive to have as a housekeeper.
HILARY. And what about you? What'll you do the next two or three months?
VICTOR. I shall cross the days off a calendar and hope you're having bad weather, and Charles is getting on your nerves.
HILARY. That's not very kind.
VICTOR. I feel angry, jealous, indignant and unhappy, but certainly not kind. But there it is. Marriage isn't like a tray of *hors d'oeuvres,* you can't just pick what you fancy. You've got to take the lot or nothing.
HILARY (*brightly*). Well, it's all settled, then. (*Rises, crossing to* L. *of him.*) I'm sorry you were wounded. Is it very painful?
VICTOR. Yes, it is a bit now.
HILARY. I think it was simply wonderful of you to fight a duel over me, it really was very romantic and I'm terribly touched. (*Very close to him.*) And very grateful.
VICTOR. For what?
HILARY. For missing Charles.
VICTOR (*crosses below her to* L. *of her*). If you're going to talk like that I'll be sorry I did.
HILARY (*her face almost touching his*). Aren't you going to kiss me good-bye? (*Pause.*) But then of course according to you, we shan't know for a couple of months if it really is good-bye, shall we?
    (*She is interrupted by the entrance of* CHARLES *by* D.R. *below armchair to on stage of it.* HILARY *and* VICTOR *move apart rather guiltily.*)
CHARLES. He'll be here in a few minutes. He followed us in his own car, so he could get home again. How are you feeling now?
VICTOR (*crossing to chair chaise longue*). Charles, we've talked the whole thing over, and I've decided—
HILARY (*sits on* R. *arm of sofa*). No, darling, I've decided. Victor's idea is that I should come away with you for three months, at the end of which time he hopes I shall return to him.
    (VICTOR *sits on chair chaise longue, feet on stool.* CHARLES *crosses up to level with sofa.*)
CHARLES. Having got bored with me.
HILARY. Exactly.
VICTOR. Come now, I didn't put it quite as crudely as that, did I?

CHARLES. I'm sure you did. But why fight a duel then?
HILARY. Because he couldn't be bothered to write me a letter, and was too mean to send me roses.
CHARLES. I don't understand.
HILARY. No, but the point is I do.
CHARLES. Well, I don't think you will get bored, and anyway I'm willing to chance it.
HILARY. Are you, Charles, are you? (*Rises and comes to on-stage end of stool chaise longue.*) Victor, d'you remember Beulah?
VICTOR. She's not lost again, is she?
CHARLES. Who the hell is Beulah, and what's he got to do with it?
HILARY. Beulah is a doll belonging to Emma, whom she has loved devotedly for years. (*Sits on stool back to* VICTOR.) You can always tell how much a doll is loved by its state of dilapidation. Beulah is maimed and nearly bald, and over the years she's had a lot of trouble with her eyes. About two Christmases ago Emma was given a new doll, and she christened her Angela. Angela had real hair you could permanently wave, if you wound her up at the back she could recite "Now I lay me down to sleep" when she was put to bed. And she was very beautiful. And the inevitable happened. (*Rises to face fire.*) Well, about six months ago Emma had her tonsils out. As she was getting into the car to go to the hospital clutching the beloved Angela under her arm, she suddenly stopped dead and said, "Where's Beulah?" And she wouldn't go without her, do you remember, Victor? We searched for an hour and Beulah was eventually found in a summer house, damp, discarded, rather mouldy and covered in ants. We soaked her in Dettol, wrapped her in a towel, pinned a label to it saying "Emergency Ward" and Emma stopped crying. It's a commonplace, rather sad little story that must have happened to hundreds of children in hundreds of households. I'm sorry to have repeated it. Particularly as I'm old enough to know better. (*Turns to fire.*)
CHARLES. And what happened to Angela?
HILARY. I'm ashamed to say (*She is very ashamed.*)—she was left behind. Face downwards—on the gravel.
VICTOR. If this story is supposed to illustrate what, I think, are your intentions, I must warn you I'm in no mood to be soaked in Dettol. (*Throws hot-water bottle on to sofa.*)
CHARLES. Well, I guess I pick my face out of the gravel. And leave by the same door I came in by.

(HILARY *crosses to* CHARLES *below sofa and embraces him.*)
HILARY. Oh Charles! Dearest Charles, I'm so sorry. So deeply sorry. But when I saw Victor in this—this wounded state, I suddenly realized—no, not realized, remembered—I suddenly remembered how very much I love him. I'd forgotten it for a whole week.
VICTOR. You should write it down on your shopping list.
HILARY (*to below sofa*). And I'm afraid I don't want to leave him, not for three months or even three hours. There it is. (*Sits on stool of chaise longue.*)
CHARLES (*to* VICTOR). You were right—weren't you?—and I guess you've proved your point.
VICTOR. About what?
CHARLES. Duelling and the divorce rate. You could never leave a husband who'd fought and been wounded for you, could you, Hilary?
(HILARY *shakes her head.*)
Goddamit! I knew it! (*Breaks* U.S.) Why in hell didn't I miss you, what a sucker I've been—what a goddam sucker.
VICTOR (*rises to ring bell*). Now you mustn't say that, Charles.
HILARY. What are you doing, darling?
VICTOR. Ringing the bell.
HILARY. You can't do that, Sellars will be in bed, it's much too late.
VICTOR (*back to sit in chair of chaise longue*). No, no, he won't. He's much too over-excited to go to bed; besides he's tearing up his novel. As a matter of fact, Charles, I reckoned on your trying to miss me when you fired.
CHARLES. But I was absolutely certain I had.
VICTOR. So I took certain measures—
CHARLES. What exactly do you mean?
HILARY. What measures could you take?
VICTOR. Perhaps precaution is a better word.
(*Enter* SELLARS, *doing up his dressing-gown, to* R. *end of sofa.*)
SELLARS. You rang, milord?
VICTOR. Yes, Sellars, I did.
SELLARS (*crosses slowly to on stage of stool chaise longue*). Excuse my dressing-gown, milady.
VICTOR. As you and I anticipated, Sellars, Mr. Delacro intended to miss me when he fired. He's a little put out and can't quite understand how I came to be wounded. You'd better tell him what actually happened.

SELLARS (*turns to* CHARLES, *who has dropped to level with him*). I marked his lordship, sir.
CHARLES. Marked! What do you mean, marked?
SELLARS. It's a technical term in duelling; when they used rapiers they used to say pinked. We reckoned what with the excitement and tension you'd be too preoccupied to notice, sir. I fired from the hip.
CHARLES. Do you mean to tell me—?
SELLARS. That I shot his lordship. Oh yes, sir, on his instructions of course, sir.
HILARY (*rises to above chaise longue*). Victor, is this true?
VICTOR. Oh yes, darling.
HILARY. And I thought it was all so romantic. Victor, I could kill you.
VICTOR. Sellars might well have saved you the trouble. He shot very poorly at the practice this morning. Ask Hattie.
HILARY. Hattie! Do you mean to tell me she knows all about this?
VICTOR. Oh yes, of course. What was the best you did, Sellars?
SELLARS. Three flower pots out of five, milord.
HILARY. Three flower pots out of five.
SELLARS. Will that be all, milord?
VICTOR. Yes, thank you. Good night, Sellars.
SELLARS Good night, milord.
  (*His exit* D.R. *is interrupted by the entrance of* HATTIE, *who wears a magnificent mink coat.* HILARY *sees her immediately as she comes in, crossing below arm-chair to* C., *leaving door open.* SELLARS *goes out.*)
HATTIE. Victor darling, how are you feeling now?
HILARY (*shouting*). Where d'you get that coat? (*Crosses below* HATTIE *to* R. *of her.*)
HATTIE. Someone gave it to me.
HILARY. What for?
HATTIE. To keep me warm, I suppose.
HILARY. Who gave it to you?
HATTIE (*ignoring this*). I've been dying to show it you. Aren't you jealous?
HILARY (*looking at* VICTOR). D'you know for a split second I was. I really was.
HATTIE. Well, I can't blame you. (*Goes right round* HILARY *showing it off.*) Isn't the colour dreamy?
HILARY. Take it off.
HATTIE. D'you want to try it on?

HILARY. I have tried it on. Take it off.
HATTIE (*below sofa*). I can't, darling, I haven't much on underneath.
HILARY (*round R. end of sofa*). I couldn't care less, take it off.
HATTIE. I'll let you try it on in the morning.
HILARY (*sees gun on sofa table*). Take it off.
HATTIE. Really, darling, I can't.
HILARY (*picking up revolver*). I'm going to count three. One—two— What d'you do, just pull the trigger? (CHARLES *pushes her hand round to window as she fires. There is a smash of glass.*) Ah yes, that's it, now then, for the last time, take it off.
HATTIE. I suppose this is what's called being frightened out of your skins. (*She lets the coat fall to the ground and stands, looking very attractive.*)
HILARY. Give it to me.
        (HATTIE *picks up the coat and hands it to her.*)
Dearest Charles, thank you. It's the most lovely coat I've ever seen, but I'm afraid I've got to return it to you. (*Handing it back.*)
HATTIE (*picks up hot-water bottle*). I'm cold!
CHARLES (*handing her the coat*). Then I guess you'd better put this on again.
HATTIE (*in ecstasy*). Oh Charles! (*Crosses to him and gives him hot-water bottle and puts on coat.*) Thank you. Isn't it gorgeous!
VICTOR. Useful, too.
HATTIE (*sits on sofa*). Oh, isn't it wonderful? I've got a mink! It just goes to show, doesn't it? Hil darling, you must have looked lovely in it.
HILARY. Well, I liked it, I must say, but it's a little too much for a housekeeper to wear mink.
HATTIE. What do you mean, housekeeper?
HILARY. That's my position here for a little while.
HATTIE. Thank you, Charles.
CHARLES. You're welcome, ma'am. (*Drops hot-water bottle in armchair.*)
VICTOR (*rises to L. of* HILARY *and takes her hand*). And so are you welcome, my darling.
        (HILARY *does a bob curtsey.*)
HATTIE. Oh well, if there's going to be curtseying— (*She curtseys to* CHARLES, *sinking right down to the floor.*)

CURTAIN

PROPERTY PLOT

Act I, Scene 1

SET

On desk
    Telephone, U.S. end
    Note pad (full), D.S. of telephone
    A.B.C., on side of telephone
    Cheque book (full), top U.S. drawer
    Account book (open), C.
    Biro, on account book
— Large money bag (with small bags of money in it), D.S. of account book
    Ink stand, C. off stage side
— Small money bag (empty), between account book and ink stand
— Three small money bags (full), U.S. of account book
? Three piles of eight half-crowns, on side of three full bags
    One pile of eight half-crowns, on account book
    Pile of booklets, D.S. on stage corner
    Lighter, above booklets
    Calender, D.S. off-stage corner
    Ash tray, D.S. of ink stand

Under desk
    Waste-paper basket

Against pillar above D.R. door
    Coronation chair

Against pillar on stage of U.L. door
    Coronation chair

On drinks table
— Two tonic waters (filled with water)
— Gin
    Whisky
    Soda syphon
    Two ginger ales
— Jug of water
    Angostura bitters (full)
— Four tumblers
— Four pink gin glasses
    Bottle opener
    Ash tray

On sofa table
    Ash tray
— Empty cigarette box

SET
  On mantelpiece
    Spare half-crown (for HILARY), in bowl D.S. end
    Board of lists, D.S. of clock
    Clock, C.
    Ash tray, U.S. of clock
  On floor L. of sofa
    The Times
  Under U.S. end of desk
    HILARY's shoes
  On U.L. door
    "Private" notice
  In fireplace
    Hearth brush, D.S. end
    Poker, D.S. end
  Plugged in wall below fireplace
    Electric lead for coffee pot
  On R. window sill
    White vase of pink and yellow blossom
  On D.L. table
    Blue and white vase of daffodils
  Fire-guard
    In front of fire
  Window stool
    On U.S. marks
  Logs
    Re-set from fire to log basket
  Curtains
    Open, hooked back with ties
  Window
    Open wide
  D.R. *door*
    Shut
  U.L. *door*
    Open wide to see notice
  Bell
    Above fire
  Check
    Tape
  Check
    Panatrope
    Telephone bell
    Cue lights
    Glass crash
    Mink coat

G.I.G.–F

PROPERTY PLOT

SET
  Off R.
    Copy of *Henley*
    Mushroom gloves
    Corkscrew (for SELLARS in case champagne cork won't come out)
    White cloth
    Two champagne glasses
    Bottle of champagne
    VICTOR's dressing gown
    Coffee tray with four cups and saucers, four spoons, sugar bowl and spoon
    White tin bowl with cotton wool, bandage, scissors
    Bunch of keys
    Box of matches
    CHARLES' spectacles
    VICTOR's spectacles
    Old suitcase with telephone directories, three cricket pads, four quoits, cricket bat, string of flags with each end selo-taped to side of case etc., etc.
  In prop room
    Hot-water bottle, filled in interval
    Coffee pot, coffee made in interval
    Games of "Scrabble"
    Letters O and K
    Peppermints
    Brandy
    Kümmel
    Six brandy glasses
    Four kümmel glasses
  Off L.
    One Lüger unloaded
    One three-eight loaded for VICTOR to take on
    Two blanks loaded, fired off stage
    Bottle of blood
    Cotton wool

ACT I, SCENE 2

Strike
  Henley and coat from armchair
  CHARLES' hat and camera from chaise longue
  Glass from sofa table
  Two coronation chairs
Reset
  Henley off D.R.
  Desk chair to face slightly U.S.
  Window stool two inches D.S. of marks
  Cigarette box on sofa table
Check
  Whisky
  Gin
  Tonic

Soda
Ginger ale
Water
Angostura
Four pink gin glasses
Four tumblers
Curtains open
Windows open
Doors shut
Cuckoo

ACT II, SCENE I

Strike
  Dirty glass from desk
  Dirty glass from sofa table
  Everything from drinks table except ash tray and bottle opener
  HATTIE's bag, hat, gloves and scarf from chaise longue
  Both flower vases

Reset
  Sofa to face fire
  Chaise longue stool to front of sofa
  Window stool to its U.S. marks
  Chaise longue chair turned a little U.S.
  Fire guard to above log basket

SET
— "Scrabble" board with letters on it on stool
  Chaise longue with edge of board over L. edge of stool so that HILARY can kick it off.
  Letters O and K in U.S. end of fireplace
  "Scrabble" box and lid under stool
  Peppermints on floor D.S. of stool
  Six letters under L. edge of sofa
  One letter under chaise longue
  Two letters under R. edge of sofa
— Brandy, kümmel, six brandy glasses, four kümmel glasses on drinks table
  White vase with magnolia in it on desk
  Blue and white vase with daffodils and irises on D.L. table

Check
  Logs in basket
  Miniatures
  Coffee tray (coffee made)
  Keys
— Old suitcase
  Hot-water bottle filled
  Curtains open
  Windows shut
  Doors shut
  Fire alight

PROPERTY PLOT

Act II, Scene 2

Strike

Coffee tray and peppermints from stool chaise longue
Coffee cups from mantelpiece
Brandy bottle from drinks tray
Dirty glasses from mantelpiece and sofa table
Suitcase and all its contents

SET

VICTOR's coat over back of sofa (glasses in pocket)
CHARLES' coat over desk chair (glasses in pocket)
SELLARS' coat on desk

Reset

Chair chaise longue to Act One marks
Window stool to D.S. marks
Brandy to off U.L.

Check

Four pistols off U.L.
Blood-stained shirt off U.L.
Victor's dressing gown
Cotton wool
Scissors
Bandage
Hot-water bottle
Soda water
Champagne
Two glasses
White cloth
Curtains closed
Windows closed
D.R. door closed
U.L. door open

PERSONAL PROPS

VICTOR

Two cigarettes
Collect dressing gown
Collect four half-crowns

HILARY

Half a crown
Collect her shoes

HATTIE

One cigarette
Cigarette holder
Claridges' matches

PROPERTY PLOT

CHARLES
  Hat
  Camera
  Light meter
  Booklet
SELLARS
  Matches
  Spectacles

FURNITURE PLOT

Pink and white upright chair outside D.R. door
Half-circle table (D.R. table) between D.R. door and D.R. pillar
Coronation chair against D.R. pillar
Pink armchair on stage from D.R. door
Desk below R. end of window U. and D.S.
Satinwood armchair with two figures C. back (desk chair) in front of desk
Embroidered stool (window stool) below C. window
Round mahogany table (drinks table) below L. window
Coronation chair against pillar on stage of U.L. door
Sofa L.C.
Kidney-shape table (sofa table) behind sofa
Small tray-top table (D.L. table) between D.S. of fireplace and built-in cupboard
Chaise longue chair and stool D.S. of D.L. table

STAGE DRESSING PLOT

Large white and gold vase bottom shelf of D.R. table
Pair of smaller white and gold vases each end of D.R. table
Gold lamp stand with white shade and red and white tassel C. of D.R. table
Small gold ash tray on D.R. table
Black pillar with bronze bust on it R. of R. window
White bust R. end of C. window-sill
Small bronze bust R. end of L. window-sill
Large white and gold case L. end of L. window-sill
White and gold pillar L. of L. window
Blue white and gold lamp-stand with white shade and blue tassel on white and gold pillar
Log basket U.S. of fireplace
Fender in front of fire
Shovel U.S. end of fender
Poker, tongs and hearth brush D.S. end of fender
Fire guard in front of fire in side fender
Magazines under drinks table
White and gold lamp stand with black and gold shade U.S. end of D.L. table
Blue, pink and white china ash tray C. of D.L. table
Flower vase D.S. end of D.L. table
Lots of small china figures and two small floral china pots in D.L. built-in cupboard
Four cushions on sofa

Mantelpiece U.S. *to* D.S.

1. Blue, white and gold jar with gold lid
2. Candle light fitting
3. Black and white china jar
4. Two invitation cards behind black and white jar
5. White miniature in gold frame
6. Rust, white, green and blue china ash tray
7. Female sphinx ornament
8. Clock
9. Male sphinx ornament
10. One invitation card behind clock
11. Two cards behind male sphinx
12. Round bronze ash tray
13. Candle light fitting
14. Blue, white and gold jar

COSTUME PLOT

HILARY

Act I, Scene 1

Blue and white striped blouse
Light beige corduroy tailored trousers
Light brown water-proof zip jacket
Pale blue ankle socks
Light brown flat shoes

Act II, Scene 1

White watered silk evening dress with black piping, and a pink rose on the front
Black satin evening shoes

Act II, Scene 2

White silk nightdress
Green chiffon dressing gown
White slippers with coloured embroidery on them

HATTIE

Act I, Scene 2

Tangerine coloured woollen dress
Matching hat
Beige suede shoes
Beige fabric gloves
Large beige hand bag
Coloured chiffon scarf

Act II, Scene 1

Gun-metal coloured tight-fitting evening dress
Jacket to match
Evening shoes to match

Act II, Scene 2

Dark mauve all-in-one pyjamas
Light mauve satin dressing gown
Dark mauve high-heeled bedroom slippers

PROPERTY PLOT

ACT II, SCENE 2

Pale pink camiknickers
Mink coat
Shoes belonging to evening dress

VICTOR

ACT I, SCENE 1

Light brown cord trousers
Blue woollen shirt
Red tie
Brown tweed jacket
Brown leather boots
Pale blue socks

ACT I, SCENE 2

Same as first scene except for a pale blue cardigan instead of tweed jacket

ACT II, SCENE 1

Green velvet smoking jacket
Black evening trousers
Cream evening shirt
Black bow tie
Black evening shoes
Black socks

ACT II, SCENE 2

Same as previous scene minus smoking jacket and shirt changed for an identical one with blood on left sleeve

CHARLES

ACT I, SCENE 1

Blue American style suit
White shirt
Red tie
Grey socks
Black shoes
Grey felt hat

ACT II, SCENE 1

Black dinner jacket
Black evening trousers
White shirt
Black bow tie
Black socks
Black evening shoes

ACT II, SCENE 2

Same as previous scene minus coat

SELLARS

ACT I, SCENE 1

Morning coat
Striped trousers
Black waistcoat
White shirt
Black tie
Black boots

ACT I, SCENE 2

Same as first scene

ACT II, SCENE 1

Black evening trousers
Black alpaca jacket
White shirt
Black bow tie
Black socks
Black shoes

ACT II, SCENE 2

Same as previous scene minus coat

ACT II, SCENE 2

Black evening trousers
Woollen dressing gown
Brown corduroy bedroom slippers

Milton Keynes UK
Ingram Content Group UK Ltd.
UKHW020831230924
448677UK00021B/41